La Belle

The Ship That Changed History

La Belle
The Ship That Changed History

Bullock Texas State History Museum

James E. Bruseth, Guest Curator
and
Catalog Editor

Guest Essays by

Juliana Barr James E. Bruseth
Jeffrey Durst William C. Foster
Jesús F. de la Teja Toni S. Turner

**Published for the Bullock Texas State History Museum
by Texas A&M University Press**

First edition

Manufactured in China by Everbest Printing Co., through FCI Print Group
This paper meets the requirements of ANSI/NISO Z39.48–1992 (Permanence of Paper).
Binding materials have been chosen for durability.

Library of Congress Cataloging-in-Publication Data

La Belle : the ship that changed history / exhibition organized by Bullock Texas State History Museum ; James E. Bruseth, guest curator and catalog editor ; guest essays by Juliana Barr . . . [et al.].
p. cm.
Exhibition catalog.
Includes bibliographical references.
ISBN 978-1-62349-033-1 (pbk. : alk. paper)
ISBN 978-1-62349-084-3 (e-book)
1. La Salle, Robert Cavelier, Sieur de, 1643–1687—Exhibitions. 2. *La Belle* (Frigate)—Exhibitions. 3. Shipwrecks—Texas—Matagorda Bay—Exhibitions. 4. Underwater archaeology—Texas—Matagorda Bay—Exhibitions. 5. Matagorda Bay (Tex.)—Antiquities—Exhibitions. I. Bruseth, James E. II. Barr, Juliana. III. Bullock Texas State History Museum.
F392.M4L3 2013
917.64'13204—dc23 2013004516

Distributed by Bullock Texas State History Museum and
Texas A&M University Press

This publication accompanies the *La Belle* special and permanent exhibit installations at Bullock Texas State History Museum

Catalog design by Sara Thaxton, Graphic Composition, Inc., Bogart, GA

Catalog photography by Jay B. Sauceda

Custom illustrations and maps by Ralph Appelbaum Associates

La Belle artifacts shown in the catalog are the property of the Musée national de la Marine, Paris

Cover illustrations courtesy Texas Historical Commission.

Frontispiece: *La Salle's Louisiana expedition in 1684,* Oil on canvas by J. A. Théodore Gudin, ca. 1844. Courtesy © RMN-Grand Palais / Art Resource, NY

BULLOCK TEXAS STATE HISTORY MUSEUM
TheSTORYofTEXAS.com

TEXAS HISTORICAL COMMISSION
real places telling real stories

Musée national de la Marine
Paris – Palais de Chaillot

Contents

Foreword

For more than twenty years, Texas Historical Commission (THC) archaeologists searched for La Salle's lost ship, *La Belle,* in the shallow murky waters of Matagorda Bay. On a warm June day in 1995, THC divers under the supervision of then-THC State Marine Archeologist J. Barto Arnold III, located a shipwreck containing historic artifacts of European origin. The first cannon to be lifted from the waters bore late seventeenth-century French insignias, proof that the ill-fated *La Belle* had at last been found.

To safeguard the wreck from storms and treasure hunters, in 1996 the THC embarked on a full-scale excavation of *La Belle* under the direction of then-THC Archeology Division Director, Dr. James Bruseth (also Guest Curator for the *La Belle* exhibit at the Bullock Texas State History Museum). Using a cofferdam to conduct an unprecedented dry excavation of a shipwreck in the middle of the bay, our archaeologists successfully unearthed the remains of the ship and its cargo. Our partners at Texas A&M University's Conservation Research Laboratory ensured the expert preservation of more than one million artifacts recovered from the wreck.

Like La Salle's expedition, the impact of this archaeological investigation extended far beyond the borders of Texas. After completing the excavation of the vessel, the French Republic officially claimed *La Belle*, citing archival documents listing the ship as one of King Louis XIV's vessels. Under the United Nations Convention of the Law of the Sea, a flag state (in this case, France) maintains ownership of a governmental vessel lost on a non-commercial venture. Accordingly, France argued that *La Belle* was on an official mission for the king when lost, and therefore was still owned by the French Republic. The U.S. State Department agreed, and an international agreement was negotiated by the French Republic, the U.S. Department of State, the Musée national de la Marine, and the THC. The document was signed on March 31, 2003, giving ownership to France but allowing the ship and its contents to remain in Texas under the control of the THC. The agreement also assigned responsibility through a separate accord to the Musée national de la Marine (Musée national) in Paris to work with the THC on issues related to curation, research, documentation, and exhibition of *La Belle*. The wreck and all of its artifacts are actually part of the Musée national's collection. French authorities have expressed their full support for the Bullock Museum's exciting new exhibit.

We are very proud of our contributions to the La Salle shipwreck project and are delighted by the Bullock Museum's bold vision for displaying *La Belle* as the centerpiece of the central atrium. The new installation will immerse museum visitors in the dramatic story of seventeenth-century exploration and colonization along the Texas coast in a way it never has before. By exploring how these events impacted not just the French colonists but also the broad sweep of Texas's indigenous and European history, the exhibit offers a unique opportunity to tell the real and fascinating story of France's failed attempt to gain a foothold on the northern Gulf of Mexico. And our partnership with Texas A&M University, the Bullock Museum, and the Musée national de la Marine will yield benefits to scientists, scholars, and the general public in Texas and across the world for generations to come.

Mark Wolfe
Executive Director, Texas Historical Commission

Preface

The Bullock Texas State History Museum was in the planning phase as the initial recovery of *La Belle* began. Within a year of the ship's excavation in 1995 and 1996, Lieutenant Governor Bob Bullock began to promote an initiative to build a Texas state history museum in Austin. By the following biennial session of the state legislature, funds were appropriated to build a museum and the design phase began. During that period, the importance of *La Belle* was recognized and a recommendation was made by the museum's leadership to design the building to display *La Belle* permanently once preservation treatment of its hull and artifacts was completed.

From the very beginning, the Texas State History Museum Foundation has been a vital partner in the vision and mission of the Bullock Museum. By providing private funding, the Foundation has consistently supported quality, dynamic learning experiences for more than six million visitors of all ages since the museum opened its doors in April 2001.

Along with our current and previous Foundation board members throughout the state, I applaud the museum for the *La Belle* initiative and share in the excitement of what this new permanent exhibit will mean for Texas and our many visitors. We thank our generous donors for their continued financial support. Under the leadership of board presidents Michelle Brock, Clay Johnson, and Brian McLaughlin, the Foundation, through its many donors, has achieved new goals in supporting the museum. The *La Belle* project would not have been possible without the support and hard work of the Foundation's staff members throughout the campaign.

The arrival of *La Belle* marks the next chapter in the museum's own history, one that all Texans and museum visitors can embrace and celebrate. Special thanks to the State Preservation Board and to the Bullock Museum's dedicated staff. Collectively, these talented professionals have made *La Belle* a reality.

Jan Felts Bullock
Honorary Chair
Texas State History Museum Foundation

Introduction

When the French arrived on the Texas coast in 1685, a series of events played out that would change the course of history. Today *La Belle* is an important touchstone to that story, helping us understand the region's role in the larger context of international history. The discovery, excavation, and preservation of *La Belle* offer a new and broader understanding of the people and social forces that shaped Texas's cultural legacy. The story of La Salle's expedition is one of Texas's most dramatic and exciting chapters, but it also represents state-of-the-art science and conservation technology.

During the planning phase of the project, a roundtable of noted scholars convened to further analyze the complex and significant consequences of Spain's dramatic reaction to the French incursion into Texas in 1685. With a rousing mix of archaeologists, anthropologists, and historians in the room it was clear that the story was complex, with nuanced and varied opinions of the historical events. These opinions, along with multiple interpretations of the evidence, are reflected in the scholars' essays chosen for this catalog. Our interpretive goal is to bring to the forefront a balanced story of the complex encounters between American Indians, the French, and the Spanish that greatly influenced the course of history in a region that represents two-thirds of the United States.

Since the discovery of *La Belle* there have been several key players and supporters of the endeavor to bring the ship's story to light. On the institutional level, the Texas Historical Commission has been at the helm for nearly twenty years guiding the recovery, conservation, and stewardship of the ship with unprecedented methodology, approach, and scope. The Conservation Research Laboratory at Texas A&M University's Center for Maritime Archaeology & Conservation has successfully performed a mammoth undertaking in preservation treatment.

We wish to thank the citizens of the state of Texas and organizations including the Texas State Legislature, the Texas State History Museum Foundation and its board, and the Friends of the Texas Historical Commission, who have all helped to bring this ambitious project to fruition. We wish to recognize the Odyssey Museums that represent the Gulf Coast communities of Corpus Christi, Port Lavaca, Victoria, Bay City, Rockport, Edna, and Palacios, who have made important contributions to the project. We also thank the many scholars and advisors, with a special thanks to Dr. Jim Bruseth for his passion and dedication to the project overall and his depth of knowledge about this incredible story. Dr. Jesús F. de la Teja and Dr. Juliana Barr have provided crucial insight as scholar advisors. We also wish to recognize our collaborations with the Musée national de la Marine in Paris who, seventeenth-century records confirm, remain the actual owners of *La Belle* and its contents.

Finally, thank you to the entire staff of the Bullock Texas State History Museum and our close colleagues at the State Preservation Board under Executive Director John Sneed. The expertise and commitment of the hundreds of staff members created a thoughtful interpretation of a complex history.

Victoria Ramirez, *Deputy Director*
David Denney, *Director of Special Projects,*
Bullock Texas State History Museum
Austin, Texas

In late 1683 the French explorer La Salle sought support for an expedition to North America amid European national rivalries and political intrigue.

European Competition for the New World

JESÚS F. DE LA TEJA

On classroom maps, the seventeenth-century contest for empire seems straightforward. Different colors represent the colonial boundaries of Spain, France, Portugal, and England at any given point in history. A Western way of looking at the world, it is a convenient fiction that masks both how little of the vast expanses claimed by each nation these countries actually controlled and how ignorant they were of the peoples who had made the Americas their home for thousands of years.

It is a fiction built on medieval legalistic principles, themselves based on ancient Roman law and Catholic Christian belief. When Pope Alexander VI issued his famous Bull (papal decree) *Inter cætera* in 1493, which Spain and Portugal followed up in 1494 with the Treaty of Tordesillas, the carving up of the planet among the Atlantic kingdoms of Europe began in earnest. The logic was flawless—that is, if you were an Iberian Christian: God, through his son Jesus Christ, had given spiritual dominion over the globe to Peter, whose religious descendants, the popes, exercised absolute authority over spiritual matters. Because the peoples of the "New World" were ignorant of the One True Faith, the pope designated the monarchs of Spain as his agents to carry out the work of salvation. Of course, the Spanish Crown and its vassals who carried out this evangelization were entitled to compensation, and thus the pope gave them dominion not just over the peoples of the New World but over its territory as well.[1]

Neither France nor England was entirely convinced by Alexander's Bull, nor by the Treaty of Tordesillas. They were, however, more than happy to accept the notion that the aboriginal inhabitants of the Americas had less right to the lands they had inhabited for millennia than did whatever European kingdom was able to defend a claim to territory "discovered" by its agents. In fact, England and France were not all that late to the game; their explorers and fishing fleets had acquired a good sense of the North Atlantic region around Newfoundland by the first decade of the sixteenth century. In the long run, the problem for Spain's

Illustrated map of the Americas
This map shows how fifteenth-century Europe divided up the "New World." The Catholic Pope Alexander VI issued a papal decree in 1493 dividing the Americas between Spain and Portugal. Spain was granted all of the Americas to the left of the dotted line, while Portugal was given the tiny sliver of South America to the right of the dotted line. The Treaty of Tordesillas in 1494 moved the dividing line westward (solid line), thus giving Portugal a little bit more of South America. Neither France nor England were included in this division of land.

Taking Possession of Louisiana and the River Mississippi, in the Name of The Louis XIVth, by Cavalier De La Salle. Color lithograph by Jean-Adolphe Bocquin, ca. 1860. By the late seventeenth century, France was Spain's most dangerous rival in North America. In 1682, Robert Cavelier, Sieur de La Salle, discovered that the Mississippi River flowed into the Gulf of Mexico and he claimed all the land drained by the river for King Louis XIV of France. *Courtesy The Historic New Orleans Collection, Acc. No. 1970.1.*

rivals proved to be that while the Spanish soon capitalized on their successful conquests of the Aztec and Inca empires and the discovery of rich veins of silver, the territories explored in North America by the French and the English (and even Spaniards like Coronado and De Soto) appeared to lack both sophisticated civilizations and precious metals. Thus, neither the voyages of the Italian Sebastian Cabot for the English in the 1490s through the 1500s, nor of the Frenchman Jacques Cartier in the 1530s through the 1540s generated sufficient excitement to produce permanent settlement.[2]

Rather, by the second half of the sixteenth century, both the French and the English had settled on an informal policy of poaching on the Spaniards. Pirates and privateers (pirates operating under royal license) of both nations captured hapless Spanish cargo ships and raided coastal towns, but made no formal attempts to directly challenge Spanish rule. The unsuccessful French Huguenot effort to establish a colony at Charlesfort, South Carolina, in 1562—which Spain considered a piratical and heretical encroachment—resulted in an expedition under Pedro Menéndez de Avilés and the founding of St. Augustine, Florida, in 1565. Thirty years later, partly acting on rumors of renewed English efforts to open a Northwest Passage and partly on other rumors of a rich Indian kingdom in the interior of the continent, the Spanish Crown authorized Juan de Oñate to carry out the 1598 occupation of New Mexico.[3]

As a field of European imperial contest, then, North America did not become important until the seventeenth century. Overextended and underfinanced (even with the

***Carte de la Nouvelle France et des pays voisins* (*Map of New France and neighboring countries*), ca. 1696**
This 1696 French manuscript map of North America, attributed to Guillaume Delisle, shows Spain's continued dominance in the region after La Salle's expedition. The map depicts the lower Mississippi Valley and adjacent regions as part of "Floride," as Spanish possessions between New Mexico and the Atlantic were known at the time. *Courtesy Library and Archives Canada/Maps, Plans and Charts/NMC6351.*

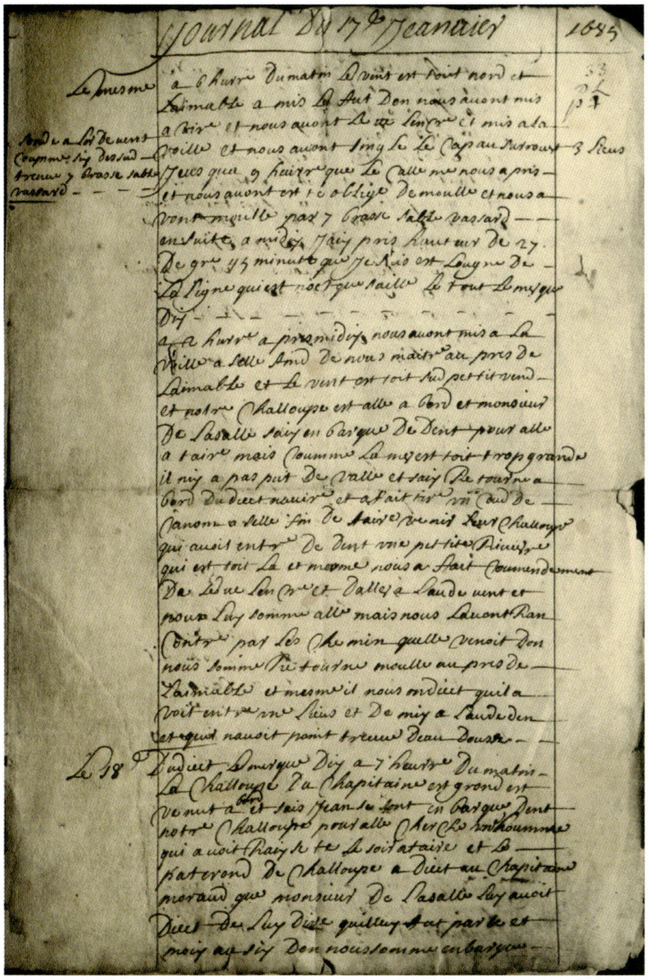

***La Belle*'s logbook, January 1685**
A logbook is a journal kept by a ship's captain or pilot. It records the daily distance and direction sailed and any other important nautical information about travel, such as weather conditions. One page of *La Belle*'s logbook is pictured here. A total of four pages of *La Belle*'s logbook exists today in the Archivo General de las Indias in Seville, Spain. The Karankawa took the logbook when they ransacked Fort St. Louis in the winter of 1688. They gave four pages of the book to visiting Jumano, who carried them to Spanish authorities in Nueva Viscaya, or New Spain. From there the pages eventually made their way to the official archives in Seville. The pages served as evidence to the Spanish that the French were encroaching on their territory. *Courtesy L'Archevêque (Jean) Items, di_05687, di_08876, The Dolph Briscoe Center for American History, The University of Texas at Austin.*

wealth of the Indies at their disposal), Spain's rulers could do little to stop the English from beginning the occupation of the North American Atlantic seaboard and the French from establishing themselves in Canada. Even Sweden and Spain's arch-nemesis, Holland, managed to establish North American colonies before being driven off by the English. Increasingly weakened by shortsighted dynastic struggles in Europe, particularly the long and costly Revolt of the Netherlands, the successors to the Spanish King Phillip II (the first monarch to claim an empire on which the sun never set) also experienced European encroachment in the Caribbean, including: English occupation of Barbados in 1627 and conquest of Jamaica in 1655; French occupation of Guadaloupe in 1634 and conquest of St. Croix in 1650; and Dutch occupation of Aruba and Curaçao in 1634.[4]

By the late seventeenth century, France had developed

into Spain's most dangerous imperial rival in North America. In Europe, France had overcome internal religious and political upheavals to emerge as the continent's most powerful nation by the reign of Louis XIV. His father's powerful minister, Richelieu, had already started France on the road to global power by fostering the country's interest in Asia and North America. In 1627 the king authorized the Company of New France (Company of One Hundred Associates), which was given rights over North America north from Florida. Although the company eventually failed (as did England's two Virginia companies), it laid the groundwork for making French Canada a growing concern. The company's extensive and expanding trade network drove exploration of the interior at the same time that Jesuit missionaries and traders cemented alliances with many of the peoples with whom they came into contact. French farmers and artisans, although never as numerous as their English counterparts along the Atlantic seaboard, created nuclei of French settlement.[5]

Despite their success in establishing permanent colonies in the New World and intercepting the bulk of Spanish silver—either through direct capture or by supplying Spanish markets with the majority of their manufactured goods—both France and England were interested in accessing the wealth of the Spanish Indies more directly. Robert Cavelier, Sieur de La Salle, was one of the French explorer-traders who had helped extend French interests into the Great Lakes region. When he returned to France in 1683 with the news that the Mississippi River connected New France and the Gulf of Mexico—commonly considered the "Spanish Sea"—a world of opportunities presented itself to Louis XIV and his ministers. La Salle himself may have been interested in establishing a settlement at the mouth of the great river from which to trade directly with Spanish colonials, but for French policymakers such a colony also represented a base from which to launch the conquest of the opulent silver mines of Mexico.

The fiasco that was La Salle's 1684 expedition nevertheless changed the imperial landscape of North America. Spain was forced to renew its attention to the upper Gulf of Mexico region, and although it did not settle Texas permanently for another quarter-century, it did occupy Pensacola in 1698. France returned to Louisiana in 1699, gaining control of the northern Gulf coastal region from Mobile, Alabama, to Natchitoches, Louisiana, in the first two decades of the eighteenth century. It was the founder of Natchitoches, the Quebec-born Louis Juchereau de St. Denis, whose 1714 arrival at Presidio del Río Grande (present-day Guerrero, Coahuila) led directly to the permanent Spanish occupation of Texas in 1716.[6]

La Salle's expedition to North America set sail in 1684 with 400 soldiers, sailors, and colonists, and the supplies needed to build a colony.

La Salle's 1684 Expedition

WILLIAM C. FOSTER

In the summer of 1684, Robert Cavelier, Sieur de La Salle, was ready to sail from France to the New World. French King Louis XIV gave him authorization to establish a colony on the Mississippi, but La Salle received only partial financial assistance from the king for his colonial adventure. To fully fund his expedition, he gambled that he could trade with Native Americans for furs and hides, to be exported back to France and sold. Supremely confident in his plan, La Salle even borrowed the additional money he needed from French money lenders at interest rates up to 150 percent.[1]

He departed in the summer of 1684 from La Rochelle on the west coast of France with a large expedition of about four hundred soldiers, sailors, and colonists. The expedition party sailed aboard four ships led by the warship *Le Joly*, followed by the small frigate *La Belle*, the storeship *L'Aimable*, and the small ketch *Le Saint-François*. The plan was to first visit the Caribbean island of Saint-Domingue (modern Haiti) and then sail south of Cuba into the Gulf of Mexico and toward the mouth of the Mississippi River. Louis XIV supported La Salle's plans to establish a fort and a colony on the lower Mississippi. But the king had another—and secret—mission for La Salle: to obtain information on the rich Spanish silver mines in Nueva Vizcaya (modern Chihuahua, Mexico). The king anticipated an invasion of the area to capture Spain's mines and to obtain New World silver for France.[2]

La Salle's expedition included his faithful friend, Henri Joutel, who served as unofficial chronicler, post commander, and chaperone for six French teenage girls brought to establish the colony's first families. In addition, a strong clerical contingent of six priests was aboard, including La Salle's older brother, the Abbé Jean Cavelier, and the priest Anastase Douay, both of whom would later return to France with Joutel and prepare separate expedition accounts.[3]

The decision to dispatch the 1684 expedition was finalized only after La Salle had briefed the French king and court on his expedition conducted two years earlier from the Great Lakes down the Mississippi River, discovering the mouth of the river as it flowed into the Gulf of Mexico. As related to the court, La Salle's expedition party left the Great Lakes, moved down the hard-frozen Illinois River, and arrived at the free-flowing Mississippi in early February 1682. Continuing down the river, the party arrived in mid-March at the mouth of the Arkansas River and met the

Portrait of La Salle, ca. 1879
Courtesy Histoire de Cavelier de La Salle, *di_08875, The Dolph Briscoe Center for American History, The University of Texas at Austin.*

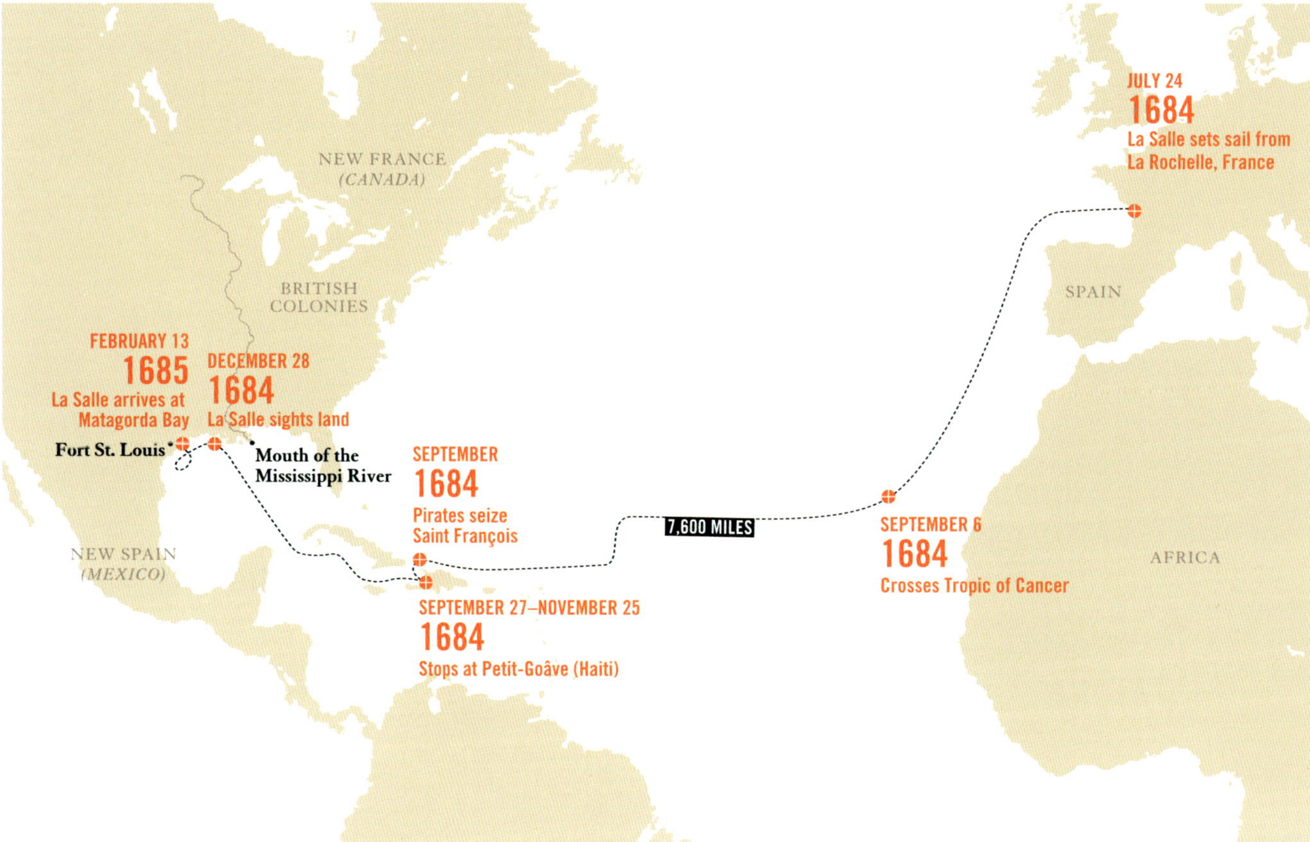

Illustrated map of La Salle's route

La Salle left France with four ships in the summer of 1684. The group sailed southwest to harness the Atlantic trade winds, and then sailed to the Caribbean Islands and northwest across the Gulf of Mexico, first sighting the coast on December 28, 1684. Ironically, the spot where La Salle first sighted land is far closer to the actual Mississippi River than where he finally landed his expedition.

friendly Acansas Indians, whom the Frenchmen Jacques Marquette and Louis Jolliet had visited on their trip down the river in 1673.[4]

With help from the Acansas, La Salle's party canoed farther downriver, beyond the amicable Taensa and the villages of the more aggressive Natchez Indians, to the lower channels of the Mississippi. There in late April, La Salle formally announced and registered his claim for France's dominion over the Mississippi River and all lands drained by the river and its tributaries. In May and early June of 1682, La Salle canoed back upriver to his Acansas friends. According to several French chroniclers, the Acansas served the Frenchmen watermelons, pomegranates, and peaches, which originated in the Old World, but whose seeds had probably come to the Acansas via a series of native trade routes from Spanish mission areas in northern Mexico. By mid-July the expedition party was back on the Great Lakes.

In late 1683 La Salle sailed from Canada back to France to meet with the king and his court, and to present his discovery and his plans for a new expedition to the Mississippi. La Salle initially had difficulty obtaining the king's support and had to rely on two abbots, Claude Bernou and Eusèbe Renaudot, who had special favor with the king. They helped La Salle prepare a plan that impressed the king, who agreed to support him. La Salle was to command the expedition on land, but while at sea, Taneguy Le Gallois de Beaujeu, captain of *Le Joly*, was in charge of the ships. This arrangement caused dissatisfaction between the two men, and their relationship deteriorated to the point that they communicated mostly by letters.

La Salle was uncertain about how he would reach the Mississippi River. He considered a route that would bring him back to New France (today's Great Lakes and eastern Canada) and sail up the St. Lawrence River. From there he could travel across to the Illinois River and then reach

La Belle's "ship kit" markings

La Belle was originally intended to be assembled upon arrival in North America. Markings found on the timbers were instructions for how to reassemble the ship. The marking "TIIII" indicates that this frame was to be placed on the starboard side, four frames from the center of the ship. The "T" is for the French *Tribord*, or starboard side. The "IIII" represented the Roman numeral IV. However, there was not enough cargo space on the remaining ships to transport *La Belle*, so the ship was assembled in France. *Courtesy Texas Historical Commission.*

the Mississippi River. For this effort, though, he needed a ship in pieces (as *La Belle* was originally planned). He could carry the major frames with him, assemble them into a vessel in the New World, and then sail the ship down the Mississippi River.

King Louis XIV signed a royal commission at Versailles on April 14, 1684, giving La Salle the right to settle the territory drained by the Mississippi River, called *Louisiane*, and to profit from its resources. But the king's approval included an expedition to the Mississippi River via the Gulf. Further complicating La Salle's plans for bringing a ship in pieces with him, there was not enough cargo space on his ships. So *La Belle*, "the ship kit," was assembled in Rochefort, France, in two months, to be sailed as part of a fleet of ships.

Captain Beaujeu, who had control of the expedition while at sea, sailed westward across the Atlantic. On September 6 the fleet crossed the Tropic of Cancer and two weeks later first sighted land. Five days later only three ships arrived at the French port of Petit-Goâve—*Le Saint-François* was lost to pirates.

La Salle's party remained at the port from late September until late November 1684. Upon leaving the island, Joutel commented, "I believe it would have been better had we stayed there for only two or three days, just to let our sick gain strength and procure some provisions."[5] Joutel was concerned that all kinds of mischief was brewing in the port among the ship's crew, soldiers, and local buccaneers, who led several of La Salle's men astray. One, Dionisio Thomas, deserted to join the crew of a pirate ship headed to raid Spanish coastal communities on the Yucatán Peninsula.

Thomas had befriended one of La Salle's servants, and from him learned of La Salle's secret mission to investigate overtaking the rich silver mines in Nueva Vizcaya of northern Mexico. When the pirate ship carrying Thomas was captured by a Spanish fleet, the crew was taken to Veracruz for interrogation. In an unsuccessful effort to save his own life, Thomas divulged La Salle's intention to establish a fort

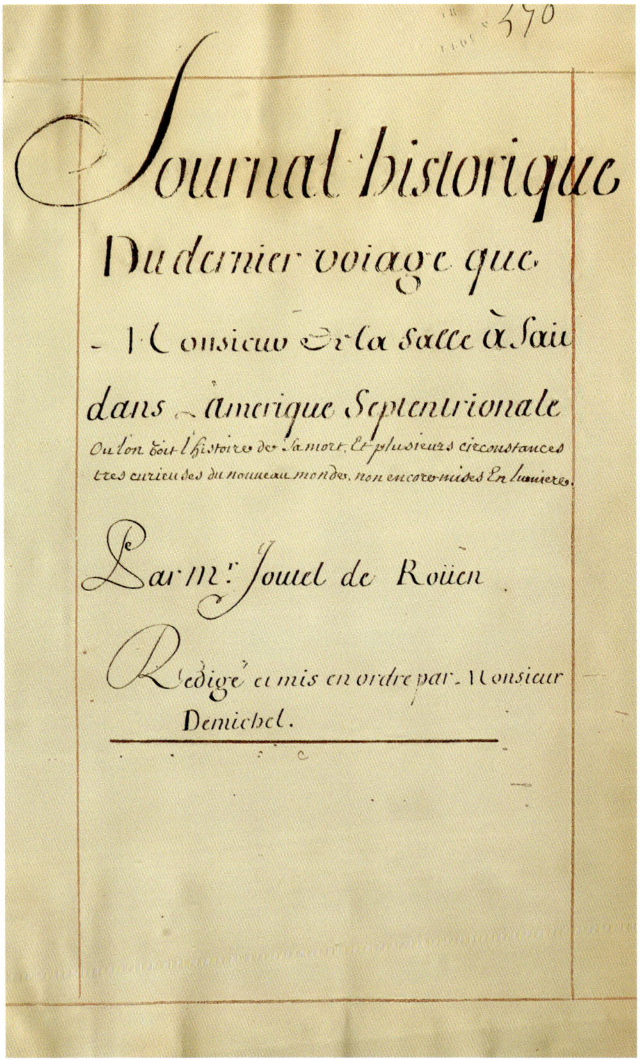
Journal historique
Du dernier voiage que
Monsieur de la Salle à fait
dans l'amerique Septentrionale
Ou l'on voit l'histoire de sa mort, Et plusieurs circonstances
tres curieuses du nouveau monde, non encore mises En lumieres.
Par Mr. Joutel de Roüen
Redigé et mis en ordre par Monsieur
Demichel.

***Journal historique Du dernier voiage que Monsieur de la Salle à fait dans L'amérique Septentrionale* (*Journal of the last voyage of La Salle*), ca. 1712**
Henri Joutel kept a journal of La Salle's last expedition in which he detailed the journey and much of what the colonists saw and experienced in their new home. After La Salle's death, Joutel eventually returned to France and published his journal in 1713. This is the handwritten copy of the journal that was subsequently typeset for printing. *Courtesy of the Trustees of the Boston Public Library/Rare Books.*

and colony near the mouth of the Mississippi. Perhaps more importantly, he disclosed La Salle's interest in the silver mines of northern Mexico. The secrecy of La Salle's voyage was thus lost to Spanish officials.[6]

The reduced three-vessel French fleet sailed south of Cuba by way of the Cayman Islands, to Cape Saint-Antoine on the far west coast of Cuba, and into Gulf waters uncharted by the French, northward toward the mouth of the Mississippi.

On the first of January 1685, La Salle briefly landed on the western Louisiana coast, which he and Beaujeu mistakenly concluded was near Apalachee Bay on Florida's west coast. Faulty maps and an inability to accurately calculate longitude probably contributed to this significant miscalculation.

La Salle sailed to the Mississippi River based on a 1684 map made by his cartographer, Jean-Baptiste Louis Franquelin. This map showed the Mississippi River flowing into the Gulf far to the west, near the mouth of the Rio Grande. Some historians have surmised that the inaccuracy of the location of the river was due to information La Salle gave his cartographer, based upon his assessment of the geography of the northern Gulf of Mexico during his 1682 expedition.[7]

Sailing westward along the Texas coast during the next several weeks exposed the colonists to the native people and the environment in which the settlement would be established. A few Indians along the beach, apparently curious and unafraid, swam out to the ships and received food, tobacco, and some glass beads. However, nothing was learned because La Salle and his men could not understand the native language. Communication was by Indian hand signs, which only later were understood and used by the French. Several days later, La Salle's Shawnee hunter, Nika, sighted a herd of about twenty bison close to the shoreline. Buffalo would become a staple in the colonists' diet.

By January 20 both La Salle and Beaujeu realized the coastline was increasingly bending southward and that they were too far west. The three ships turned around near present-day Corpus Christi, Texas, and proceeded back eastward to Pass Cavallo at the entrance to Matagorda Bay, where the colonists were to find their new home. Little did they know that the expedition had missed the Mississippi River by over four hundred miles, and that they were unprepared for the misery about to unfold in a strange and unfamiliar land.

***Vue du Port de Lacul du Petit-Goâve* (*View of the port of Lacul on Petit-Goâve*)**
Engraving by Nicolas Ponce, ca. 1791. During the journey from France, La Salle's expedition stopped at the portside town of Petit-Goâve in present-day Haiti. The town was inhabited by a mixture of French colonists and pirates, who socialized together with little regard to French law. Joutel described Petit-Goâve as a place where "the air was bad, the fruit the same, and there were a great many women worse than the air or the fruit."[8] While there, La Salle learned that his fourth ship *Le Saint-François* had been captured by pirates. *Courtesy of the John Carter Brown Library at Brown University.*

Expedition Maps

Franquelin's map of Louisiana, ca. 1684
La Salle's map of North America, made in 1684 by mapmaker Jean-Baptiste Louis Franquelin, provides one reason the expedition landed off course. Careful readings of historical documents confirm that La Salle believed the Mississippi River entered the Gulf of Mexico 530 miles west of its actual location. Seventeenth-century mapmakers continued to portray this inaccurate location of the Mississippi for several more years. *Courtesy Library of Congress Geography and Map Division Washington, DC.*

Map from *Journal historique Du dernier voiage que Monsieur de la Salle à fait dans L'amérique Septentrionale*, ca. 1712
Included in Henri Joutel's journal prior to its publication in 1713 was this hand-drawn map. It shows a branch of the Mississippi River flowing into Matagorda Bay, reflecting how La Salle viewed the geography of the northern Gulf Coast. *Courtesy of the Trustees of the Boston Public Library/Rare Books.*

***A new map of the country of Louisiana and of the river Mississippi in North America discovered by Mons. de la Salle in the years 1681 and 1686 and also of several other rivers before unknown and falling into the Bay of St. Lewis*, ca. 1713**
A different map was actually published with Joutel's journal in 1713. In this version, the Mississippi River no longer flows into Matagorda Bay, but instead is depicted north of the bay by more than 100 miles. This possibly reflected the growing realization that La Salle had significantly missed the Mississippi River when he landed on today's Texas coast. *Map Reproduction Courtesy of the Norman B. Leventhal Map Center at the Boston Public Library.*

La Belle–A Small but Beautiful Ship

***La Belle* one-twelfth scale model, ca. 2003**
La Belle was small, measuring about 54 feet in length, 15 feet in width, and had a draft of 7 feet. Glenn Greico of Texas A&M University made this ship model based upon historical documents and from archaeological evidence obtained during the recovery of *La Belle*.

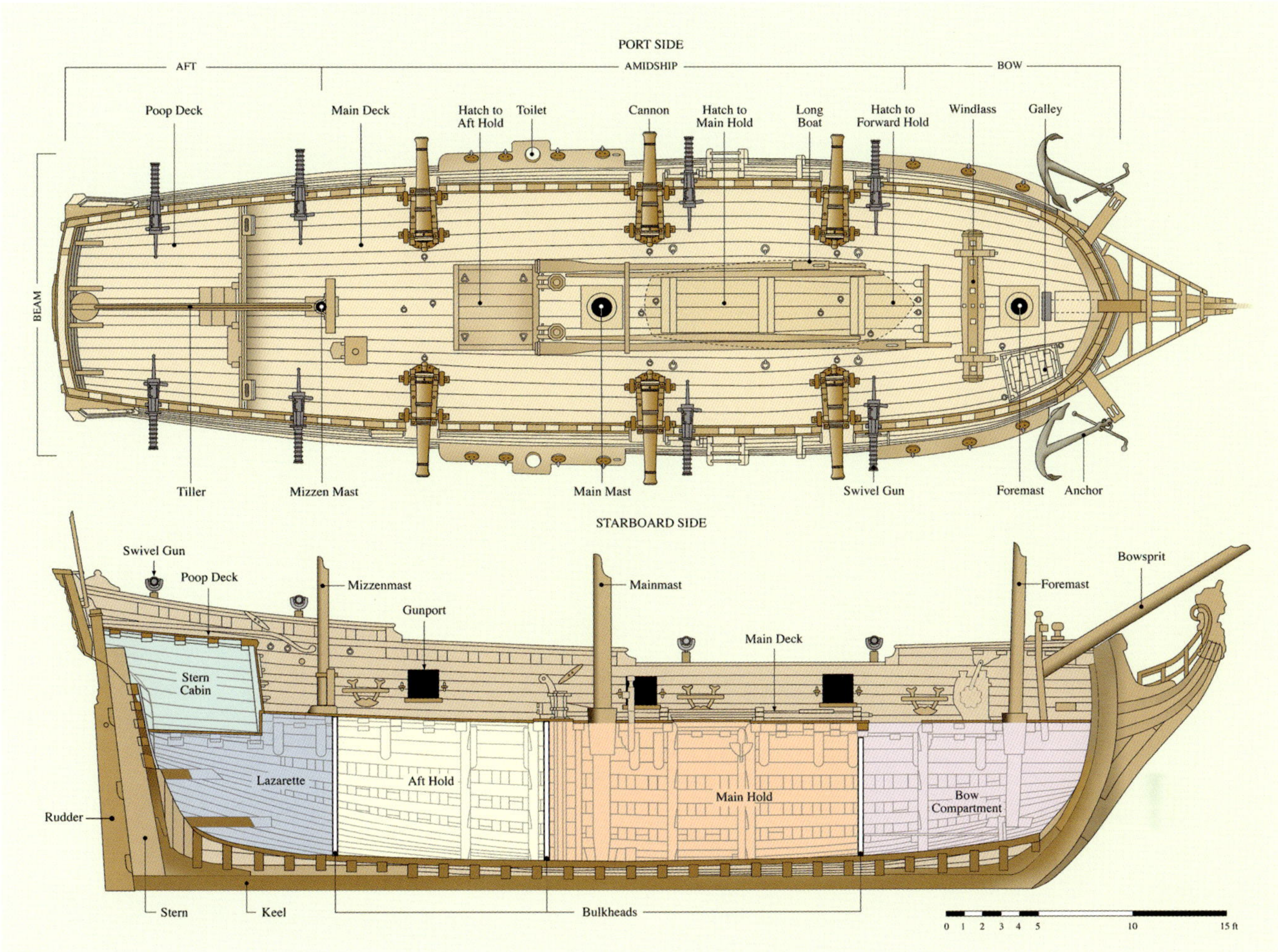

Illustration of ship compartments

La Belle was a three-masted sailing vessel, armed with six cannons and eight swivel guns for protection while at sea. The mainmast was situated slightly behind the midship frame at the widest part of the ship. The foremast was located near the bow. Both the mainmast and the foremast had two sails, each square-rigged. The mizzen mast, at the rear of the ship, had a lateen, or triangular, sail. A bowsprit extended at the bow over the water and held a small square sail. There were five compartments below deck. The bow compartment was in the front and stored excess anchor rope. It also served as some of the crew's sleeping quarters, and hammocks would have been suspended from the ceiling. Directly behind the bow compartment was the main hold. It was accessible from the deck and held the majority of the cargo. The aft cargo hold contained supplies for the colony too, but was also used by the crew for shelter from inclement weather and to play board games. Behind the aft hold was the lazarette, which held spare weaponry. Above the lazarette was the stern cabin, a small compartment that served as the captain's quarters. *Courtesy Texas Historical Comission.*

Modern illustration of *La Belle*
Illustration by Charles Shaw, Courtesy Texas Historical Commission.

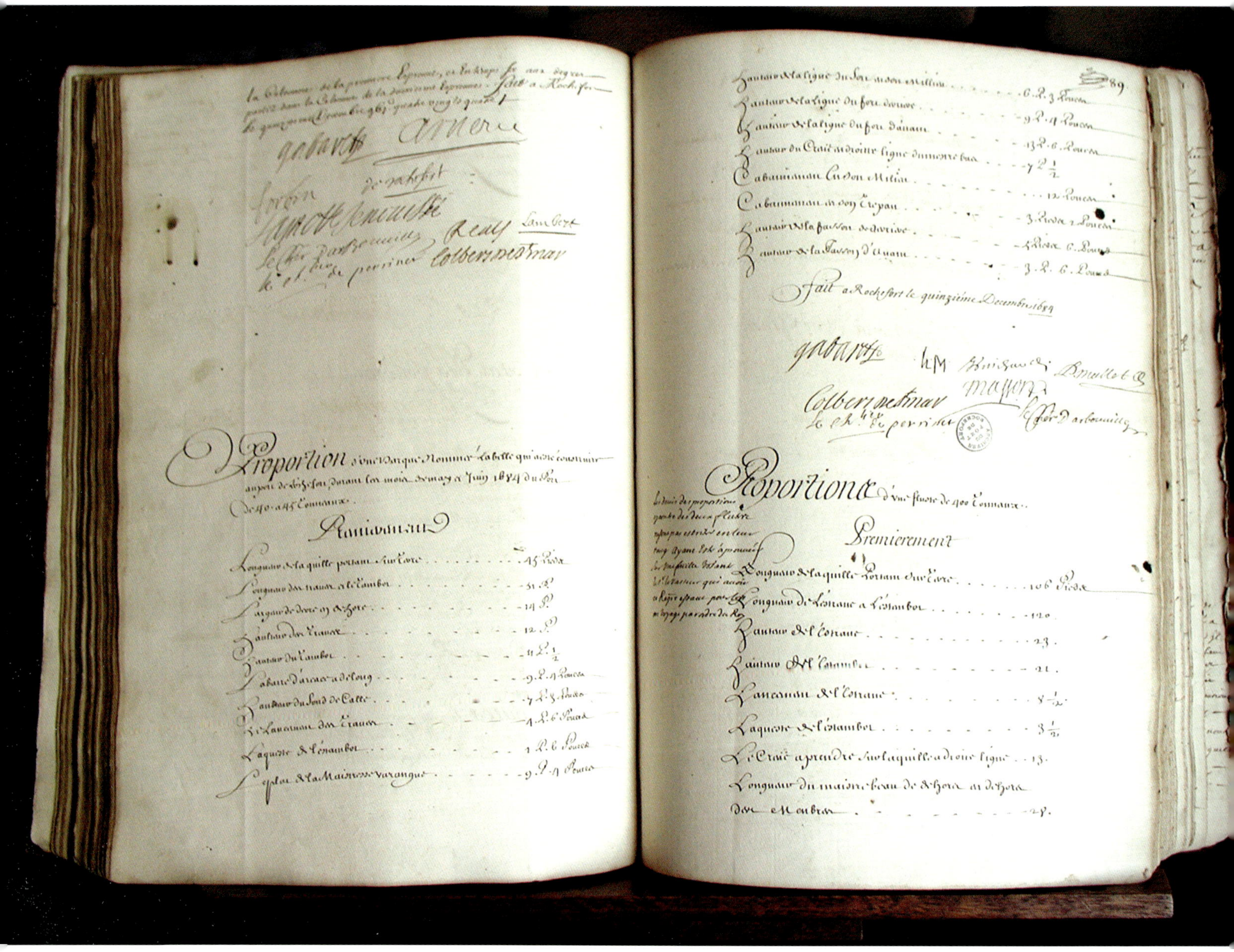

French naval ledger, December 1684

La Belle was assembled during May and June 1684. A ledger found in the naval archives in Rochefort, France, shown above, provides the original dimensions of the ship. These measurements describe the length of the hull that remains today as only slightly smaller than in 1684. The listing for *La Belle* starts midway through the page on the left and continues through the page on the right. To the right is an English translation of the document and a diagram of what the construction measurements represent. *Photo by John de Bry, Courtesy Archives du Port de Rochefort, Service historique de la Défense, Rochefort, France.*

Proportion of a barque named *La Belle* that was built at the port of Rochefort during the months of May and June 1684, of 40 to 45 tons.

1. Length of the keel	*45 feet*
2. Length from bow to stern post	*51 feet*
3. Maximum beam	*14 feet*
4. Height of stem post	*12 feet*
5. Height of sternpost	*11 feet 6 inches*
6. Maximum beam in stern	*9 feet 4 inches*
7. Depth of hold	*7 feet 3 inches*
8. Forward rake of stem post	*4 feet 6 inches*
9. After end of keel to after end of rudder	*1 foot 6 inches*
10. Mastercouple	*9 feet 4 inches*
11. Height above keel at beam maximum	*6 feet 3 inches*
12. Height of transom above keel	*9 feet 4 inches*
13. Length of bowsprit	*13 feet 6 inches*
14. Depth of Hold at Midship beam	*7 feet 6 inches*
15. Tumble home at maximum beam	*12 inches*
16. Tumble home offset between max beam & mm. stern breadth.	*3 feet 2 inches*
17. Height of deadwood at stern	*5 feet 6 inches*
18. Height of deadwood at bow section	*3 feet 6 inches*

Done at Rochefort the fifteenth of December 1684

Signed,

GABARET
HM (Honoré Mallet)
GUICHARD
P. MALLET
COLBERT de ST. MARS
MASSON
LE CHEVALIER de PERRINET
LE CHEVALIER D'ARBOURVILLE

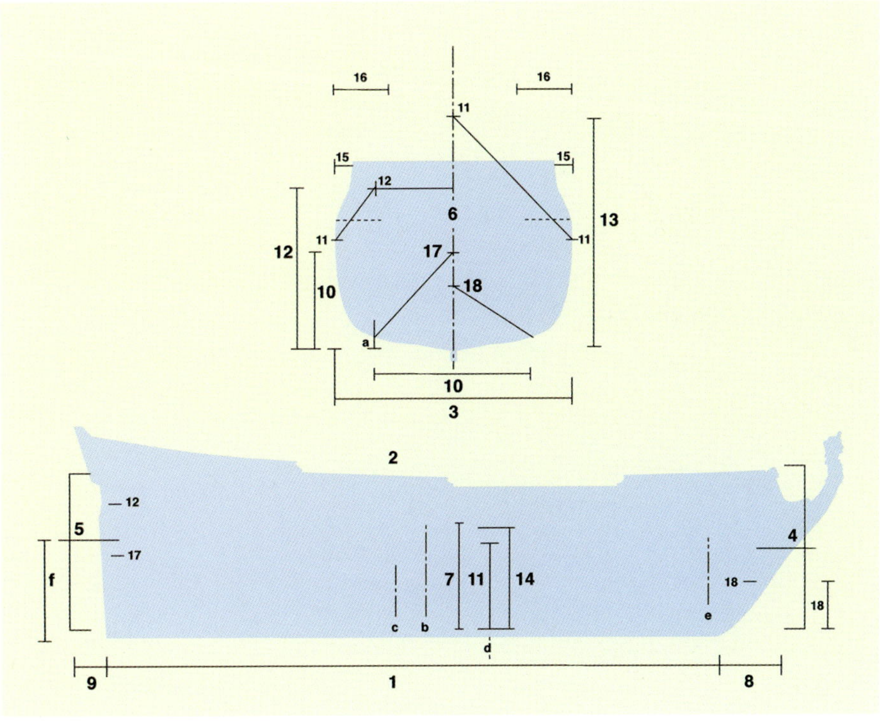

Courtesy Texas Historical Comission.

Navigation at Sea

During the voyage, the captains on the expedition relied on maps, charts, personal experience, and finely crafted instruments to navigate. They calculated latitude (north-south, on maps with lines running parallel to the Equator) easily but could not accurately determine longitude (east-west, on maps with lines running perpendicular to the Equator). La Salle instead directed the ships to the latitude where he thought the Mississippi would be. This inability to determine longitude, combined with a faulty map, led La Salle to continue sailing west, hundreds of miles beyond the Mississippi he sought.

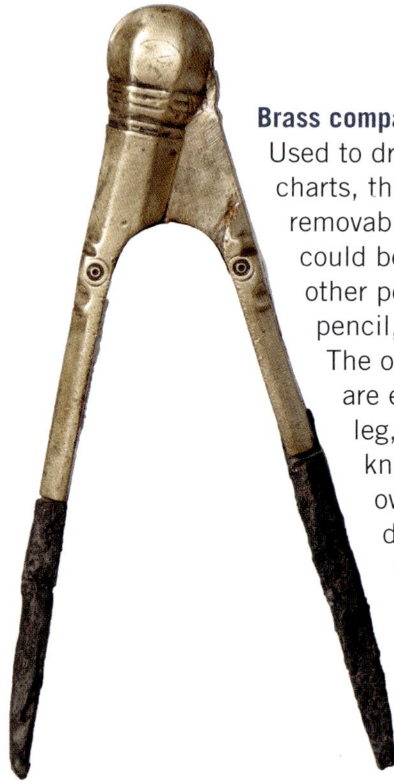

Brass compass
Used to draw on nautical charts, this compass had removable iron tips that could be replaced with other points for a pen, a pencil, or a dotting wheel. The owner's initials "IP" are etched into one leg, but we do not know the name of the owner, as the initials do not match the known crew member names. *Dimension 5.11"l x 2.5"w x .625"h*

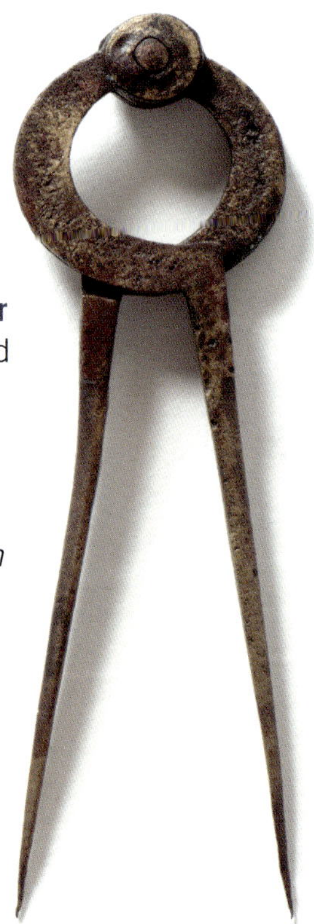

Brass chart compass divider
The pilot of *La Belle* would have used this compass to calculate the distance between ports by marking distances and dividing measurements. *Dimension 4.1"l x 1.23"w x .35"h*

Lead sounding weight
Used with a rope line to determine the depth of the water, tallow would be placed into a hole at the bottom of the weight. Sailors lowered the lead sounding weight into the water until sediment stuck to the greasy tallow inside the weight, effectively indicating to sailors where the sea floor was. *Dimension 9.5"l x 2" diameter*

Sand glass

Sand glasses were used to log the ship's speed, keep track of the time for crew member assignments, and for other purposes that required accurate timing. Sand glasses usually were designed for one hour, thirty minutes, and in some cases one minute. This example from *La Belle* would have been for thirty minutes. Typically a ship's boy would be responsible for monitoring the sand glass and turning it when needed. The page from *La Belle*'s log (see page 13) shows how this information was recorded each day. *Dimension 3.7"l x 2.36" diameter*

Gimbaled lantern

This gimbaled oil lamp would have been used for light by the captain and officers in the stern cabin. The lantern pivoted in two directions so that at sea it would be steady. When found, parts of its three wicks were still preserved. *Dimension 5.98"l x 5.98"w x 4.76"h*

Nocturnal

The nocturnal was used at night to calculate time, perhaps to within fifteen minutes of accuracy. The example from *La Belle* is one of the few ever found on a shipwreck. It is made of English boxwood and consists of three disks held together with a brass fixture that allows them to be independently rotated. A handle was attached to the larger disk and a pointer was affixed to the central brass fixture. One of the smaller disks has a calendar engraved into its face. The larger disk has a calendar, compass degrees, and constellations engraved on it. At night the North Star's position could be sighted using the pointer. Another constellation, such as Ursa Minor, would then be found. From these two sightings, and using the engraved information on the nocturnal, the evening time could be calculated. On the other side of the nocturnal is a planisphere, used for determining the constellations viewable at that time of the year. The writing on the nocturnal is in English, indicating it was probably made in England. The calendar and other information on it would have been valid for about four years, at which time a new instrument would be needed. *Dimension 9.37"l x 5.12"w x .65"h*

Sailing the Ship

La Belle under sail would have been alive with movement and sound as sails billowed and ropes and masts creaked. To harness the winds that propelled the ship, the crew constantly repositioned the sails, climbing masts and rigging to adjust the lines. The ship also required constant maintenance against wear, wind, and corrosive seawater. The crew manned pumps, mended sails, and covered ropes and rigging with protective coatings of pitch. It was hard, exhausting work.

Sailmaker's needle
This needle was used to repair *La Belle*'s sails and rigging. Maintenance of the sails and rigging would have been a daily activity and this needle would have seen constant use.
Dimension 6.88"l x 0.314" diameter

Eye hook [Cast Reproduction]
This hook was originally made of iron, and the cast shown here is made from a concretion (see page 106). A rope would have been connected to the ring; a piece of the original rope remains preserved here. Hooks like this would have been very common onboard for securing the ship's rigging and for lifting tackle.
Dimension 6.5"l x 3.125"w x 2.75"h

Ringbolt [Cast Reproduction]
Ringbolts were mounted to the ship as a place to tie ropes. Ropes for securing both the rigging and cannons would have used ringbolts. The shank of the bolt was driven into a hole bored into wood. A washer would be put over the end and then a small wedge, or forelock, would be driven into a hole at the tip of the bolt to firmly secure it in place, much like a cotter pin.
Dimension 14.76"l x 5.11"w x 2.95"h

Single block
Sailors rigged ropes and blocks to serve as pulleys that adjusted the ship's sails. A rope would run over a sheave, or pulley, inside the block. The grooves running around the ends of the block allowed it to be spliced onto the end of a rope.
Dimension 9.87"l x 7.25"w x 5.18"h

Single block, disassembled
The rigging had to be durable, so its wooden pieces were made of oak and lignum vitae, extremely hard woods. As a result, some of the blocks were so well preserved that after conservation they could be disassembled. This disassembled single block shows the internal sheave (or pulley) and the wooden pin that held the sheave in place. *Dimension 4.64"l x 3.74"w x 2.16"h*

Fiddle block
The fiddle block contains two sheaves (or pulleys), located one below the other. This type of block would have been commonly used on the bowsprit and on sail booms, places where the narrower profile of the block made for more efficient maneuvering. *Dimension 12.43"l x 5.31"w x 3.87"h*

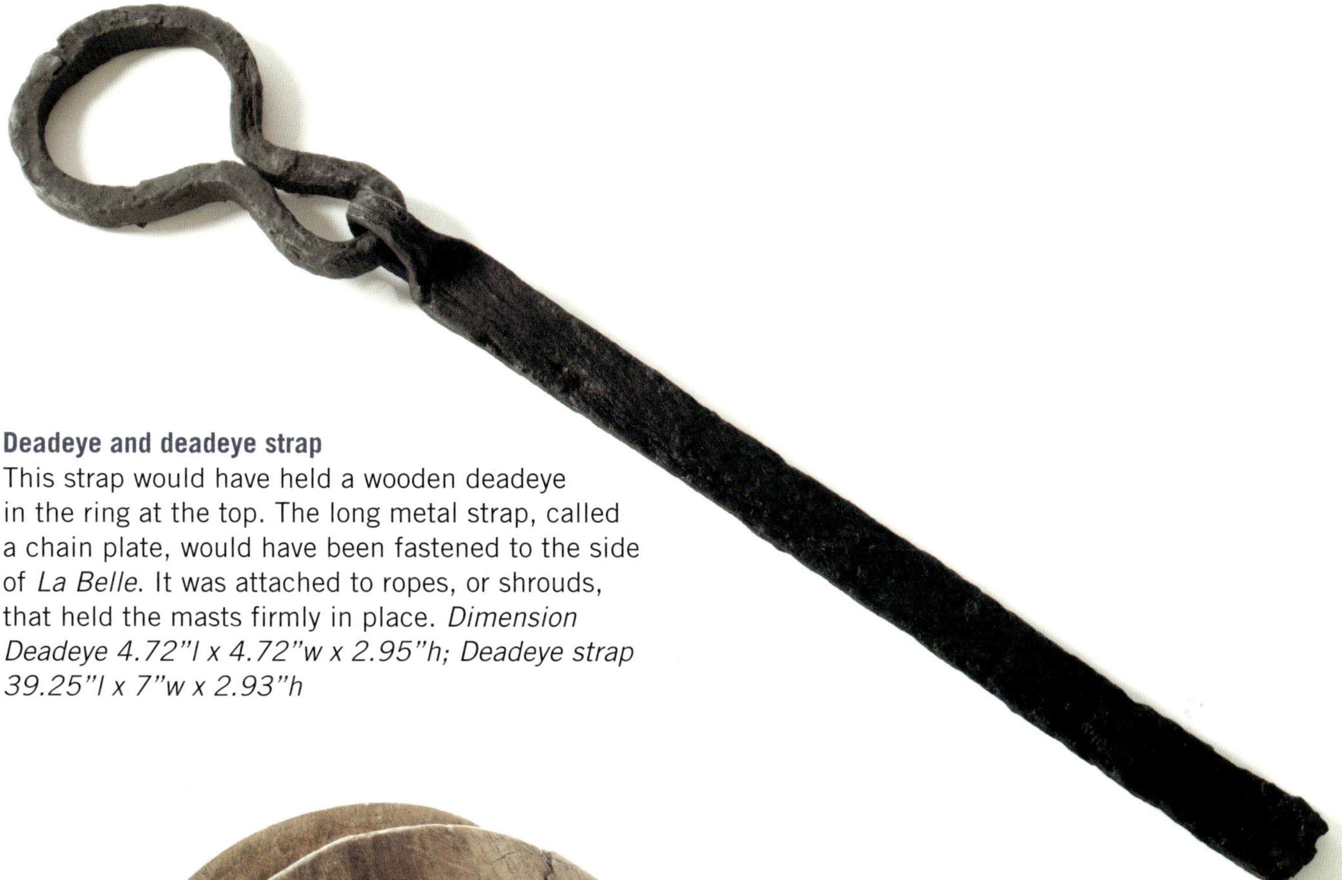

Deadeye and deadeye strap
This strap would have held a wooden deadeye in the ring at the top. The long metal strap, called a chain plate, would have been fastened to the side of *La Belle*. It was attached to ropes, or shrouds, that held the masts firmly in place. *Dimension Deadeye 4.72"l x 4.72"w x 2.95"h; Deadeye strap 39.25"l x 7"w x 2.93"h*

The Karankawa controlled the lands along the Gulf Coast when La Salle arrived in present day Texas.

Native Americans

Juliana Barr

At the time of European arrival in the seventeenth century, the landscape of Texas was criss-crossed with lines drawn between Indian groups that had long occupied the land that Frenchmen, Spaniards, and Anglos would attempt to occupy for themselves. Individual Indian group homelands brushed up against one another, their edges and peripheries creating zones of shared and contested indigenous power. Of the groups that encountered Robert Cavelier, Sieur de la Salle, in the 1680s, Karankawas found economic strength and political security in barrier islands and coastal estuaries. Caddos maintained inland ancestral landscapes that had been forged over centuries. Jumanos enjoyed territorial grasp through the mobility of their trading economies and communication networks.

Karankawa

Marine-adapted hunting and gathering groups of Akokisas, Atakapas, and Karankawas (Cocos, Copanes, Cujanes, Guapites, and Karankawas proper) held the length of the Gulf Coast. They lived in small, kin-based bands, and their territory encompassed the mainland, coast, and barrier islands. Each of the five Karankawa groups occupied clearly defined territory no matter what time of year. In the spring and summer, smaller kin-related bands dispersed throughout the marshes and prairies of the coastal plains to hunt bison, deer, and small animals, as well as to gather nuts, roots, fruits, and greens. Hunting camps located along the inland Karankawa territorial line suggest that they shared the camps with inland dwellers at the same times of the year and perhaps hunted together, though they divided the

Map of Native Americans in Texas
Texas was inhabited by numerous Native American groups in the seventeenth century. La Salle encountered the Karankawa, Caddo, and Jumano, among many other native groups, during his exploration.

Cocos
Illustration by Lino Sánchez y Tapía, ca. 1828. The Cocos, a Karankawa group, relied on the bow and arrow for hunting and fishing. The French might have learned a great deal from the Karankawa had they not angered the group by stealing their canoes. *From the collection of the Gilcrease Museum, Tulsa, Oklahoma.*

Arrow point
A single Cuney arrow point was found on *La Belle.* Its tip is broken off, which often happens during impact. Cuney points have triangular blades with barbs and were used between 1300–1700. How it ended up on the wreck is unknown. *Dimension .78"l x .51"w x .07"h*

camps into northern and southern halves for separate residency. In the fall and winter Karankawa people returned to the coast, where they gathered with others from the five groups and converged around different bays, lagoons, and barrier islands. The islands and coastal environment provided plentiful saltwater fish and shellfish as well as invaluable defensive positions for their marine encampments, isolating them from the displacement pressures that later befell other Indian groups in Texas.

With such clear boundary lines and security measures in place, it is interesting to consider the political implications of Karankawa response to the establishment of the French Fort St. Louis by La Salle's expedition in 1685. The Frenchmen erected six structures using ship timbers, poles, and mud plaster that huddled together along Garcitas Creek a league and a half (four miles) from Matagorda Bay. Three years passed before the Karankawas decided the camp had to be destroyed in the winter of 1688 and 1689. While sporadic fighting occurred between La Salle's colonists and the Karankawas, the native people appear not to have considered the French presence to be an invasion of their territory and instead shared the land and its resources with them. The animosity that existed between La Salle and the Karankawas was the fault of the French. Early in La Salle's stay on the coast, some of his men stole Karankawa canoes. These vessels were essential to Karankawa subsistence and defensive mobility between the shoreline and islands during the winter months. The theft of the canoes merited the Indians' anger and ultimately incited retaliatory raids that brought about the end of the French encampment.

Thirty-three years later, Spaniards tried to reoccupy the spot of La Salle's settlement, but their attempt met similar failure after only five years when they too violated

Modern illustration of the Caddo

The Caddo lived in a vast empire of sedentary villages, raising corn, beans, and squash, and hunting game such as white-tailed deer. La Salle traded with the Caddo for horses and food. *Illustration by Nola Montgomery, Courtesy Texas Historical Commission.*

Karankawa rules of coexistence. Thereafter no further European invasions were attempted; Karankawa geographical, economic, and political positioning afforded them much security and independence.

Historical accounts from the sixteenth through the nineteenth century all record the unvarying presence of Karankawa groups between Matagorda Bay and Corpus Christi Bay. Throughout that time, Euro-American observers consistently distinguished the five groups by language and culture, even as they regularly interacted and merged with one another in seasonal summer ranges. Archaeological and Spanish records agree in locating a major, centuries-old cultural and territorial boundary line running 10 leagues (27 miles) inland along the coastline between Karankawa lands and those of inland dwellers that remained unchanged and signified their geopolitical stability.[1]

Caddo

At the time of La Salle's arrival, the Hasinais (the "Tejas" or "Texas") and other Caddos had maintained a thriving culture in the region far northeast of the Karankawas for more than a thousand years. They had territorial stability, long-distance trading networks, and agriculturally-based communities spread thickly over an area that encompassed hundreds of miles in parts of present-day Louisiana, Texas, Arkansas, and Oklahoma. By the seventeenth century, the majority had united into three confederacies, known as Hasinai, Kadohadacho, and Natchitoches, that along with at least three other independent Caddo bands clustered in fertile river valleys of present-day northwestern Louisiana and northeastern Texas, along the Angelina, Neches, Sabine, and Red Rivers. A 1676 native report from Coahuila told of "a populous nation of people, and so extensive that those who detailed reports of them do not know where it ends." "The Coahuiles do not give more detailed reports of the Texas," the 1676 report explained, "because they say they are allowed to go only to the first pueblos of the border, since the Great Lord of the Texas does not permit foreign nations to enter the interior of his country."

Europeans would find that it took an estimated 100 leagues (270 miles) to travel from the outmost defensive perimeter, marked and guarded by hunting lodges, to the core of the Hasinai domain, on the way passing through outer villages, then ceremonial centers, before finally reaching the innermost caddis' (chiefs') complexes—all of which required several days' travel. Furthermore, they would make that trip only under escort; these were well-policed borders of a well-defended nation.[2]

The Hasinai Caddo world impressed European observers with its size, breadth, and development. It included ten villages, each of which was fifteen leagues (forty miles) long and seven leagues (nineteen miles) wide, "each very well established and in good order," every community member with his own multistructured home and lavishly productive garden, and a government so well run that it oversaw people's property and crops when they were away on business. In 1686 French priest Anastase Douay wrote with admiration about one of the primary Hasinai settlements: "This village, that of the Cenis, is one of the largest and most populous that I have seen in America. It is at least twenty leagues long, not that it is constantly inhabited, but in hamlets of ten or twelve cabins, forming cantons, each with a different name. Their cabins are fine, forty or fifty feet high, of the shape of beehives." To this European (and all others who met them), Caddos were a people "that had nothing barbarous but the name." In their own turn, Caddo leaders saw nothing to fear in their European visitors, though over time they determined that Spaniards and Frenchmen might be usefully incorporated as additional allies within their already extensive political economies by transporting Caddo trade goods in new directions and bringing new goods back to them in return.[3]

Illustration of a Jumano, ca. 1960s
The Jumano had extensive trade and social alliances with many other native groups and often served as guides, interpreters, and middlemen for the Spanish of Nueva Vizcaya, New Spain (modern Chihuahua, Mexico). The Jumano reported to the Spanish that La Salle had set up a colony and was asking about access to the Spanish silver mines. *Illustration by Frank Weir, Courtesy Frank Weir.*

Jumano

Jumanos were the ultimate traders and political go-betweens at the turn of the seventeenth century, whose professions meant they spent much of the year on the road, away from their homes. Their territory encompassed a sweeping breadth of lands from the upper Rio Grande in northern Mexico to the Southern Plains of present-day eastern New Mexico and western Texas. To the west, their settlements reached almost to Pecos, New Mexico, and to the east stretched to the Colorado River of central Texas. Across those ranges they maintained farming settlements in New Mexico and along the Rio Grande in the Big Bend region of Texas. Seasonal migrations dispersed outward from those cores to hunt buffalo, to trade, and to carry news and information long distances through Indian networks. Jumano villages could be found at natural crossroads—rivers, junctures, passes—and along native highways, serving as trading posts and communication centers. It is no wonder that so many Spanish expeditions encountered them in so many disparate places, living and traveling as they did along key riverine and overland routes throughout the region.[4]

No group was better positioned to link together native (and European) people in northern Mexico, the Southern

Plains, New Mexico, Texas, and Louisiana. They did so through long-distance trading and communication networks, making them invaluable diplomats and informants even as they helped to move commodities and natural resources from one region to another. Attending trade fairs and making annual trips between New Mexico Pueblos and east Texas Caddos, Jumanos linked together the two regions in a way that Spaniards would not be able to match for one hundred years—with a route between San Antonio and Santa Fe. The scope of Jumano trading influence increased as the Spanish began to occupy Texas. Jumanos emerged as premier horse traders, building enviable horse herds in the heartland of their territory with the ideal pasturage and watering available there, then trading them far to the east and north, to Caddos, Wichitas, and others. Their established network of contacts, mastery of trade routes and highways, and use of language—which served as a means of bridging communication among native groups—meant that Jumanos were more trusted than Spaniards to carry messages between isolated Spanish settlements.[5]

Effect of European Arrival

The borders of Jumano, Karankawa, and Caddo territories defined their interactions both with native neighbors and with Frenchmen and Spaniards who entered their lands in the seventeenth and eighteenth centuries. Most importantly, across those landscapes, Indian nations could and did exercise sovereign power within clear geopolitical borders. The Spaniards and Frenchmen who came to Texas had to build their establishments and settlements in and around native ones. Their form and location reflected not the design of imperial goals but rather the European need for and dependence upon native relationships. Europeans learned to play by the rules of Indian diplomacy and trade, they submitted in warfare against superior Indian foes, they accommodated their colonies to Indian terms for settlement within their lands, and they sought Indian alliances for their own survival. Spanish and French successes and failures in the region reflected the reality of Indian domination in Texas—something that neither European power would unseat in the years that followed La Salle's futile colonization effort.

Trade Goods

La Salle transported many items to trade with the native peoples of North America. Although King Louis XIV provided the provisions needed to establish the colony, he did not supply trade goods. These were brought by La Salle and several of the men who accompanied him. From his previous explorations of New France, La Salle understood the goods native peoples would trade for food and other items the French needed for their colony. Once the colony was established, trade goods could procure furs and hides to be shipped back to France for sale. La Salle's commission by the king granted him the right to profit from the region's resources.

During Joutel's time with the Caddo in 1687, he states, "I often went to their huts to trade, whether for corn, beans, fat, or some similar thing which the women handed over for beads, needles, pins, rings, or other objects which we might have." This quote, and subsequent quotes from Joutel, are taken from his published diary, as cited in the endnotes.

Glass beads
Chemical testing revealed that the beads were likely made in Venice. *Dimension .125" diameter*

Box of beads in situ with archaeological scale
When *La Belle* was excavated, archaeologists discovered a wooden box that contained glass beads strung together by color. The box measured 27.5 inches in length, 11 inches in width, and 11 inches in depth. It contained an astounding 618,000 seed beads, so named because of their size, equivalent to a small plant seed. *Courtesy Texas Historical Commission.*

Brass hawk bells

The Native Americans of the Gulf Coast treasured hawk bells as trade items. In native cultures, bells were sewn onto clothing and dance costumes. Today hawk bells are commonly available and are still used by Native Americans in dances. There were 1,617 brass bells retrieved from *La Belle.* Examples are shown here, and several exhibit maker's marks, such as bow ties, asterisks, and the letter "S." *Dimension .56"l x .56"w x .68"h*

In Europe hawk bells were used in the sport of falconry and tied to the legs of the bird. When the falcon, or more commonly the hawk, was flying, the tinkling of the bells allowed the falconer to know the bird's location. Often two bells of slightly different sizes were used and the difference in the tone made it easier to locate the falcon.

Courtesy Bullock Museum.

Brass rings

Archaeologists found 1,603 small brass rings on *La Belle*, commonly termed "Jesuit rings." Thirteen types of rings were found, each with a different icon or other image embossed on them. The most common image is the letters "IHS," the Christian monogram for Jesus Christ. Other images include a crucifixion scene, a female praying to a saint, Christ as a young man, "L" with a heart, Auspice Maria, the Virgin Mary, a saint holding a child, a monstrance adored by angels, Saint Francis, a female saint with a floral crown, Pietà, and King Louis XIV. Many of the rings were found in bundles, wrapped in cloth—possibly a bag—inside a wooden box, much like the one that contained glass beads (see page 42). The box measured 27.5 inches in length, 9.5 inches in width, and 9.5 inches in depth, and contained other trade items, including knives, pins, hawk bells, and small mirrors. *Dimension .81"l x .81"w x .46"h*

Brass pins

La Belle contained more than 17,000 brass pins, intended for trade with native peoples. Many were recovered in a partially preserved barrel that contained other trade items such as mirrors, knives, and glass beads. The pins were found in rows and appear to have been pinned to pieces of paper.

French pin manufacture was a relatively labor-intensive process. First, brass wire had to be cut into lengths of 1.5 to 2 inches. Then one end was sharpened and the other end was wrapped with a thin piece of wire for the head. Finally, the wire wrapped at the head was anchored by a specialized machine that stamped it to the pin.

Dimension .07"l x .07"w x .86"h

Mirror

Several dozen mirrors were packed into trade boxes and barrels. Those from the trade boxes were stored in small tin containers measuring about 2.6 inches in diameter and about .75 inch in depth. The mirrors were once coated on one side with lead to make them reflective. Their convex cross-section indicates that they were cut from a larger sphere of blown glass.

Dimension 2.36" diameter

Case knife [Cast Reproduction]
Case knives were so named because they were packed into shipping cases for transportation. In this example the blade is an epoxy cast of the original iron. A concretion or hard outer shell formed around the iron. The iron corroded away over time leaving a void. Conservators cleaned the mold and filled it with epoxy to reveal the detail of the original blade (see page 106). The wooden handle is original.
Dimension 9.8"l x .95"w x .75"h

More than 500 case and clasp knives were recovered on *La Belle*. Joutel mentions trading knives with native peoples, saying, "They are skilled at dressing . . . bison hides retaining the hair and cleaning it well. For each hide they were given a knife with which they were well pleased."

Clasp knife [Cast Reproduction]
Clasp knives were also located in *La Belle*'s cargo. These are folding knives, much like a modern pocket knife. Clasp knives were made entirely of iron. This material corroded away, but conservators have been able to find several examples that became encased in concretions before they deteriorated and have made casts of the original knives from the voids.
Dimension 5.13"l x 1.2"w x .75"h

Comb
Seventeen combs were found packed inside one of the trade boxes. The combs are made out of wood from the Rosaceae family, possibly blackthorn. On one side the teeth are spaced for combing hair; on the other side the teeth are very finely spaced for combing out lice, a widespread problem during the period. The combs from *La Belle* were both used by the colonists and stored for trade to the Indians. *Dimension 4.25"l x 2.87"w x .43"h*

Vermilion
Vermilion is a naturally occurring cinnabar pigment that was highly valued by native peoples for its intense red color. It was often used by European painters, and is highly toxic because of its mercury content. It was used as a colorant to make red paint and some groups used it to paint their faces. On *La Belle* 17.5 pounds of vermilion were found, and chemical testing revealed that the samples were diluted with iron or lead. One specimen was found inside a bark bag, which was probably how it was carried on land. *Dimension 1.5"l x 2.5"w x 3.25"h*

Axe heads

La Belle contained 664 axe heads, 558 of which were arranged in four barrels. They are all felling axes but vary considerably in size from lengths of 3.5 inches to 8 inches. The differing sizes of the axes, often found together in the same barrel, suggest that several separate blacksmiths were producing the tools, with little effort to standardize them to a common size. *Dimension 7.87"l x 3.54"w x 2.36"h*

Axe heads in situ

The axes were packed into each barrel with the blades pointed to the center and in a manner to store as many as possible in the barrel. None of the axes included handles. Cargo space for the expedition was scarce on the four ships, and La Salle knew that wood for axe handles could easily be obtained in their new homeland. He even brought along several carpenters who could make the handles. The axes would have been for use by the colonists and for trade to the Indians. Joutel comments at one point that, "They traded to the Indians . . . axes . . . for five horse-loads of corn and beans." *Courtesy Texas Historical Commission.*

Life for the French colonists was very difficult. Everything was strange and unfamiliar in their new home.

Life and Death at Matagorda Bay

JEFFREY DURST *and* JAMES E. BRUSETH

Prior to his departure from France in 1684, La Salle had encountered problems in securing able-bodied recruits for his expedition to the New World. Skilled workmen of virtually every trade were needed for establishing a frontier colony. Because they were in short supply, beggars were drafted from church steps to journey to the New World. Many of these individuals were in poor health even prior to departure and unaccustomed to travel on the high seas. Several passengers were reported to have died in passage and many of those who managed to survive the voyage were in a sick and weakened state upon arrival.

Once La Salle had selected a port on the northern Gulf Coast where his ships could be protected from both rough seas and the eyes of the Spanish and roving pirates, he or-

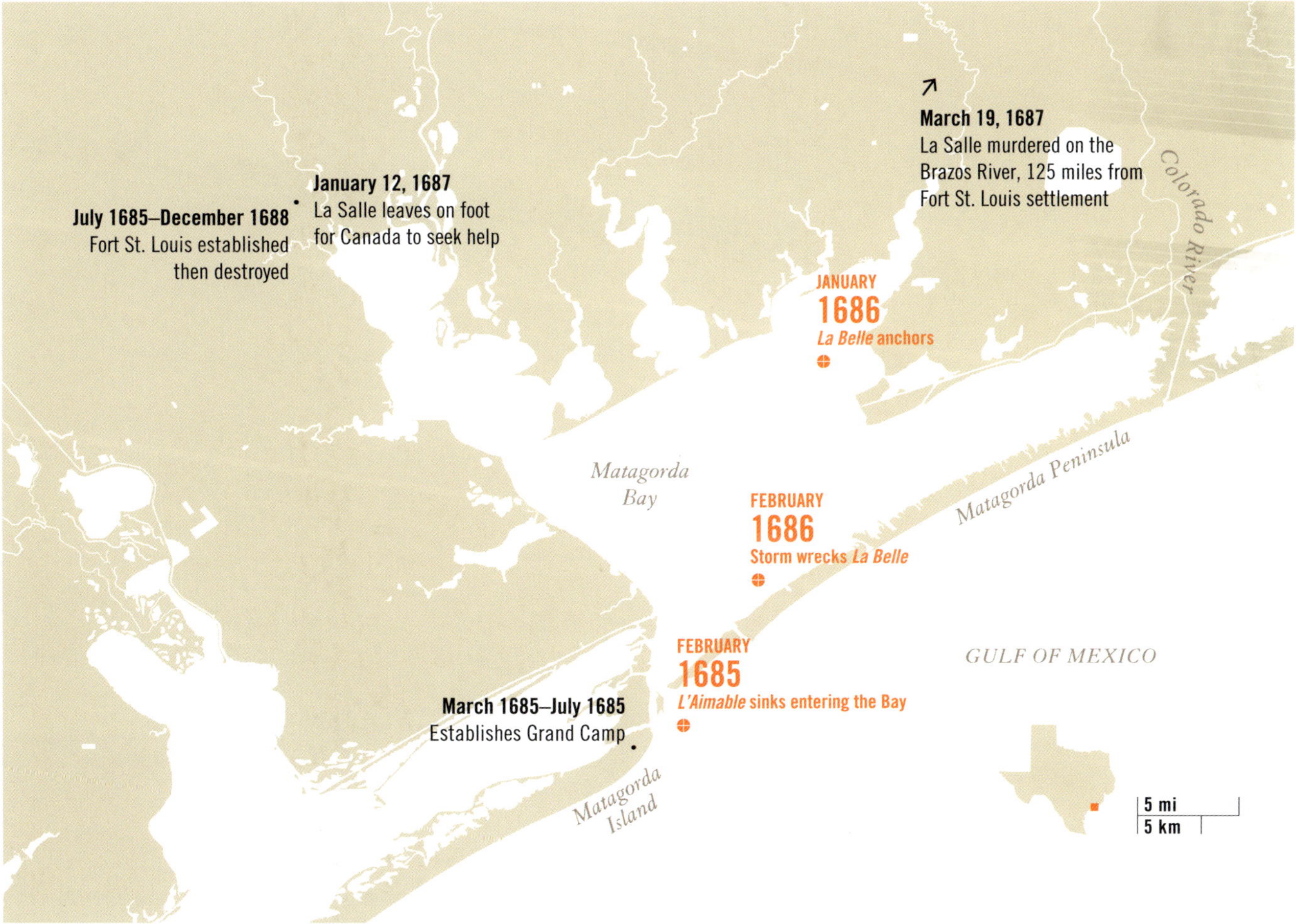

Map of Matagorda Bay, Texas, showing the wrecks of *La Belle* and *L'Aimable* and the campsites used by La Salle.

Modern illustration of *La Belle* before sinking
The cutaway of the hull reveals the cargo inside *La Belle* before it sank in 1686. *Illustration by Charles Shaw, Courtesy Texas Historical Commission.*

dered the ships to enter the bay through a shallow pass. The small frigate *La Belle* sailed easily through the pass. Unfortunately, the storeship *L'Aimable* was much larger and ran aground in the shallow waters. *Le Joly* consequently stayed outside the pass in the Gulf. The fourth ship, *Le Saint-François*, had been lost to pirates off the coast of Saint-Domingue, today's Haiti. In an attempt to salvage as much as possible from *L'Aimable*, La Salle established a temporary encampment (Grand Camp) with approximately 150 settlers on what is today known as Matagorda Island, near present-day Pass Cavallo.[1]

While La Salle was well versed in dealing with the land and the Indians of North America, very few of the settlers on board had even the faintest clue as to what they might encounter in this strange and unfamiliar new land. Their inability to deal with the native Karankawa people became evident almost immediately upon making landfall. Deadly clashes with the Karankawa—combined with the loss of *L'Aimable*, in which much of the food supplies for the colonists had been stowed—caused the situation to turn desperate quickly.

Within two weeks of making landfall on the Texas coast, approximately thirty members of La Salle's crew were either dead or unaccounted for. Within one month the number of dead or missing had risen to sixty or more. Some colonists succumbed to various sicknesses or fell victim to the Karankawa Indians, who were unhappy after La Salle's men stole their canoes. Others had eaten prickly pear fruit without first removing the tiny, hair-like spines. The spines became lodged in their throats, which then swelled to the point they could not breathe, and they ultimately died from asphyxiation.[2]

Further inland, on a high bank of a large brackish-water stream (today known as Garcitas Creek), La Salle established the location of his fledgling colony, Fort St. Louis. The colonists salvaged portions of the wrecked *L'Aimable* to construct a stronghold where La Salle and several others would reside, and where the settlers could gather when under threat of attack. A less sturdy structure was attached to the stronghold and used as a chapel where the priests

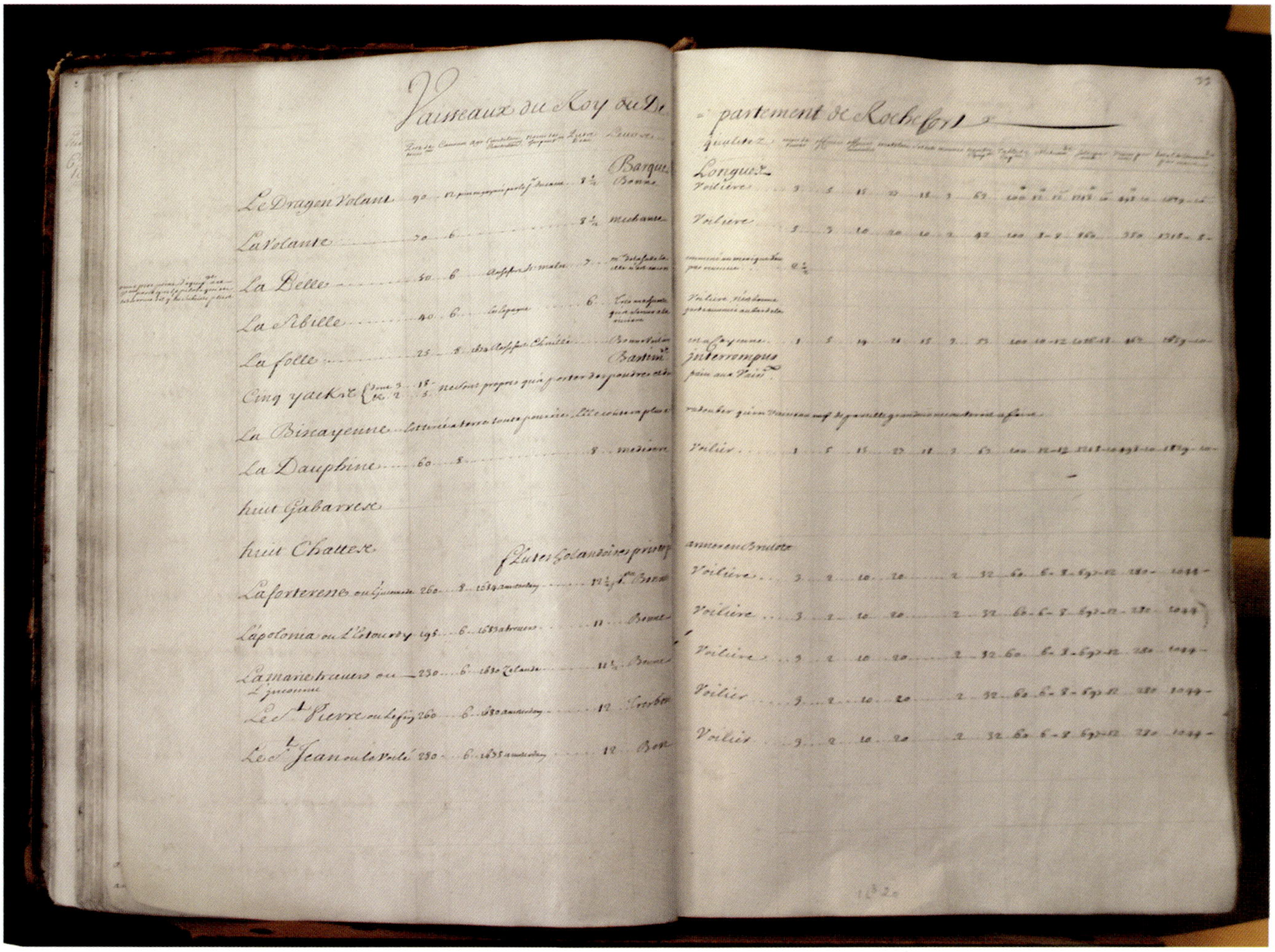

French Listing of Royal Naval Ships, ca. 1684–1689

This ledger from the French naval archives lists King Louis XIV's ships assigned to the arsenal at Rochefort, France. The third entry on the pages identifies *La Belle* as being fifty tons in size, armed with six cannons, built in Rochefort by master shipwright H. Mallet, having a draft of seven feet, and supplied with two and a half months of food. In another column the ledger notes that "Mr. de la Salle has taken her [*La Belle*] to Mexico from which she has not yet returned." At a later date, an additional notation was made to the left margin, stating, "The number of crew is not given for this vessel because the pilot has just returned and says she no longer exists." The pilot was Pierre Tessier, who became the last master of *La Belle*. Immediately before the ship's loss in 1686, Tessier was accused by his crew and passengers of being drunk most days. Having survived the shipwreck, Tessier left with La Salle a year later to walk to New France (the Great Lakes and Eastern Canada) to get help. On the way in eastern Texas, Tessier participated in the murder of La Salle. The former master of *La Belle* continued on the journey for help, eventually making his way with four other men to France, where he kept his involvement in La Salle's murder a secret. Later, Tessier traveled to Rochefort, where he gave the account of *La Belle* being lost. *Courtesy Archives du Port de Rochefort, Service historique de la Défense, Rochefort, France.*

who accompanied the colonists would conduct Mass. Several smaller and less substantial structures were placed in close proximity to the stronghold and housed the majority of the remaining colonists. Aside from the stronghold and the chapel, the Spanish later described the French structures as nothing more than small flimsy huts covered with mud and grass.

As the colonists began to settle into their new surroundings, the harsh realities of their situation became readily apparent. Wood needed for building more suitable structures was not nearby and involved risking life and limb to procure. Henri Joutel noted in his journal that more than twenty lives were lost in gathering wood for construction. Not only was the work arduous, but the Karankawa would take every opportunity to kill any colonists who strayed off alone from the others.

The newly settled colonists soon discovered that the conditions surrounding the site were unsuitable for growing many of the traditional French crops, such as lettuce, melons, and pumpkins. The plants that the colonists did manage to cultivate were often difficult to harvest because of the various vermin that competed for these same resources. Fortunately for the colonists, buffalo were usually plentiful and provided an excellent source of protein, as well as hides that could be used for clothing and for roofing their shelters.

During the time La Salle spent in what would later become Texas, he explored primarily to the east and, to a lesser degree, to the west. In late 1685, he set out for what was to become his final exploration in search of the Mississippi River. *La Belle* was now his only ship; *Le Joly* had sailed back to France after unloading men and cargo. He loaded the supplies he had left onto *La Belle* and ordered the ship to sail as far as it could to the northeast in Matagorda Bay, which he called Saint Louis Bay. The ship anchored and the crew was told to remain there while La Salle went in search of the Mississippi River. Once he found it, in about ten days, he would come for *La Belle* and sail it to the river.

Joutel's journal gives details about *La Belle*'s fate. La Salle was gone much longer than expected, and the men on the ship began to run low on drinking water. Five men were sent ashore in a small shallop to fill some barrels with water. Toward evening, the men attempted to come back to the ship, but the wind was against them and they could not make progress. Darkness fell, and the men never made it back to *La Belle*, their fate unknown. Meanwhile, those remaining on the ship killed some pigs they had brought. They did not have water for them, and they needed the food. Conditions worsened and several men even died from a lack of water.

Joutel related that the master of the ship, Pierre Tessier, took control of the brandy and wine and was drunk almost every day. Conditions reached the point where the master decided not to wait any longer for La Salle and instead to sail *La Belle* back to Fort St. Louis. In early February, 1686, the crew set off, not knowing that a powerful cold front was headed south to the bay. *La Belle* got caught in the storm and the crew lost control of the ship. The vessel dragged anchor until running aground near the southern shore of the bay. Eventually the survivors on the ship made it to shore and after three months made their way back to Fort St. Louis to tell about the loss of *La Belle*.

Two months later, La Salle returned and was confronted with the disheartening news that his only remaining ship, *La Belle*, had been wrecked during the storm. This was especially alarming because, prior to his departure to locate the Mississippi, he had ordered that *La Belle* be loaded with the supplies needed to relocate the colony to the mouth of the Mississippi. Many of the provisions that would have aided the remaining settlers in their day-to-day existence were now resting on the bottom of the bay.

Realizing that he would no longer be able to transport the colonists by sea, La Salle set off on foot headed for New France (the Great Lakes and eastern Canada), where he hoped to find help for his struggling colony. His journey was cut short when several of his own men conspired to murder the great explorer somewhere near present-day Navasota, Texas. They shot La Salle in the head and left his unburied body in the woods for the wolves to devour.

Around Christmas 1688, the remaining colonists at Fort St. Louis were attacked by the Karankawa, who killed everyone except a few children and one woman, who were taken captive. The few survivors of the failed colony lived to tell the gruesome tale of the demise of the French settlement.

Life at Fort St. Louis

La Belle easily entered Matagorda Bay, but the larger supply ship, *L'Aimable*, ran aground and sank, taking most of the colony's supplies with it. The crew salvaged what they could, using the ship's timbers to build a sturdy stronghold to safeguard their new colony, Fort St. Louis. The expedition's military escort and gunship *Le Joly* headed back to France with many crew members and colonists. Those that remained did their best to build a colony that would sustain them, but they were decimated by illness, and after stealing the canoes of the local Karankawas, they alienated their only source of help in their new homeland.

Modern illustration of pirates
La Salle established his colony, Fort St. Louis, on high ground thirty miles inland, knowing that the Spanish or pirates would soon learn about his expedition and come looking for him. In fact, pirates did look for the French settlement, but only found the remnants of the first campsite, the Grand Camp, located at the entrance to Matagorda Bay. They reported to the French on the Caribbean island of Saint-Domingue that they saw wooden grave markers showing many colonists had died. But the pirates never found Fort St. Louis, safely hidden inland. *Illustration by Charles Shaw, Courtesy Texas Historical Commission.*

Pecan tree nut
Native to Texas, pecans would have provided a source of food for the colonists. *Dimension 1.09"l x .62"w x .59"h*

Modern illustration of Fort St. Louis
Artist's reconstruction of La Salle's inland settlement, based on archaeological evidence obtained by the Texas Historical Commission. La Salle never referred to the settlement as Fort St. Louis, but rather called it the "post on the bay of Saint Louis." It was Henri Joutel, in his journal published in 1713, who first called the settlement "St. Louis"—a name that archaeologists still use today. *Illustration by Charles Shaw, Courtesy Texas Historical Commission.*

Deer antlers
These white-tailed deer antlers and partial skull were obtained by a colonist from hunting. In his journal, Joutel writes that any discussion of the local game "must begin with the bison which are very numerous, and it could be said that they were our daily bread. After bison, there are the deer, the turkey, Canada geese, other geese, swans, cranes, ducks, teals, coots, plovers, jack-snipes, sandpipers, white and brown curlews, and grouse of two kinds, one large and one small (which is the better)."
Dimension 11.85"l x 14"w x 8.46"h

Life and Death aboard *La Belle*

When *La Belle* sank during a storm in 1686, it was La Salle's only remaining ship. Before leaving to explore the coast further, La Salle ordered that the stored supplies from his colony site be transferred to *La Belle* so it would be ready to sail up the Mississippi when he returned. As a result, the little ship's hold was packed with crates and barrels when it went down. The loss of *La Belle* doomed La Salle's hopes of establishing a colony at the mouth of the Mississippi River and his plans to overtake Spain's rich mines in Nueva Vizcaya. While *La Belle* sat in the bay waiting for La Salle's return, it was essentially a floating apartment housing men and supplies. Many of the artifacts recovered speak to life aboard *La Belle* during this time.

Rat skeleton
With this skeleton discovered in the aft cargo hold, archaeological evidence from the excavations indicates that rats may have been eaten by those onboard *La Belle* just before it sank. *Dimension 1.77"l x .81"w x #".5*

Pig jaw bone
Pigs were kept on the ship while anchored in Matagorda Bay, intended for breeding at a colony site on the Mississippi River. *Dimension 4.33"l x 2.12"w x .75"h*

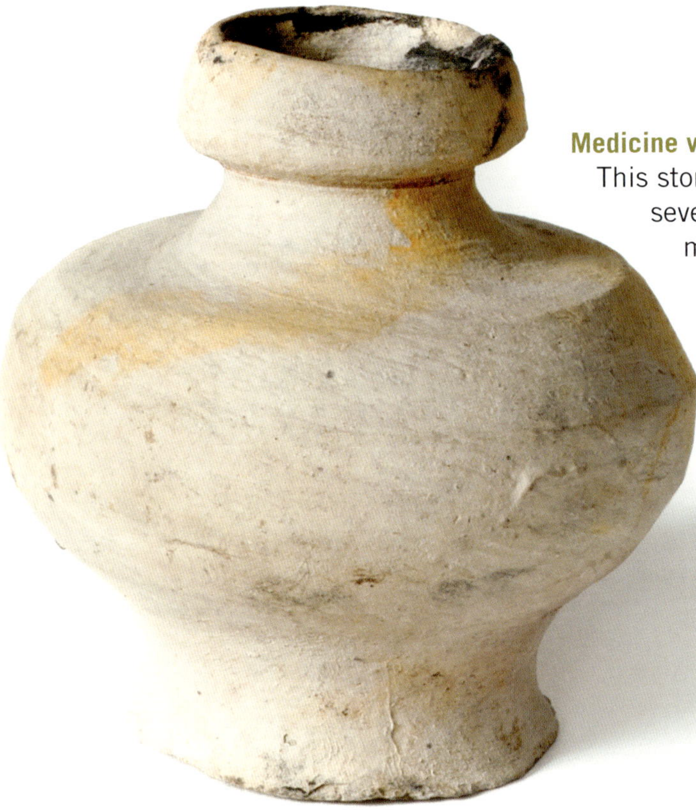

Medicine vial

This stoneware vial contained mercury, used in the seventeenth century to cure syphilis. At least one member of the expedition contracted this disease during the stay in Petit-Goâve. *Dimension 1.96"l x 1.96"w x 2.12"h*

Pewter cup

This pewter beaker has the name "Jean phily" scratched upside down on the exterior and "Phily" crudely written on the base. This item likely belonged to Jean Philix Bouillan of La Rochelle, a ship's pilot who appears on a list of sailors hired by La Salle while in La Rochelle. *Dimension 3.50"l x 2.99"w x 2.99"h*

Galley brick

Galley brick, consisting of fired clay tiles, was found in several locations on the wreck. These bricks were used during cooking and heating to keep wooden parts of the ship from becoming too hot and catching fire. A grouping from the aft hold indicates where cooking took place below deck. Another cluster in the main hold contained bricks partially covered in tar, which may have been used to heat the tar in preparation for coating the ship's rigging, a common practice on sailing ships. A third cluster was found immediately off the starboard side at the aft portion of the hull. These bricks were probably part of a small cooking area in the rear captain's cabin before the compartment deteriorated. *Dimension 7.08"l x 3.34"w x 1.03"h*

Coconut cup

While at Petit-Goâve, the colonists acquired locally made cups and bowls made of coconuts and gourds. This is a coconut cup found on *La Belle*. *Dimension 4.13"l x .3.87"w x 1.87"h*

Glass fica (right)
A fica is a good luck charm used in Mediterranean cultures, including southern France. *Dimension .93"l x .31"w x .31"h*

Game piece (above)
Gaming pieces were used for a variety of board games including backgammon. During the cold winter of 1686 the crew and passengers aboard *La Belle* took shelter in the aft cargo hold and played games to occupy their time. *Dimension 1.81"l x 1.81"w x .27"h*

Modern illustration of *La Belle* after sinking
Those still alive on the ship built a crude raft to reach land but it broke apart, killing one man. A second raft was built, allowing the colonists to go ashore, where they lived for three months until an Indian canoe washed up on the beach. The survivors used the canoe to travel back to Fort St. Louis and tell the story of the loss of *La Belle*. *Illustration by Charles Shaw, Courtesy Texas Historical Commission.*

La Salle Leaves To Get Help

In January of 1687, La Salle left Fort St. Louis with sixteen men to get help. With the loss of *La Belle*, his colony was on the verge of collapse, and he needed supplies and assistance from his countrymen. Unfortunately for La Salle, the closest place for French support was from another Fort St. Louis, located on the Illinois River at present-day Starved Rock, Illinois. This fortification was small and supplies limited. Ultimately, La Salle knew he would need to travel even further, to Montreal and Quebec, to secure additional support. While today it would be unthinkable to walk this distance, in 1687 there was no other option.

Modern illustration of La Salle's departing Fort St. Louis
Illustration by Charles Shaw, Courtesy Texas Historical Commission.

Modern illustration of La Salle's death

During the journey, somewhere near present-day Navasota, Texas, La Salle's expedition stopped to secure food. He sent some of his men ahead to obtain provisions that had been stashed away during an earlier journey. The advance party found that the food was spoiled. Fortunately, La Salle's Shawnee guide, Nika, shot two buffalo. The men stopped to smoke the meat, but soon an argument arose about who was given what portion to eat. La Salle's nephew, Colin Morenger, took control and dictated to the others who would get what portion. This was a final insult to the other men, who had endured countless hardships. That night they planned the murder of Morenger. They succeeded, and a few days later when La Salle rejoined his men, they killed him too. *Illustration by Charles Shaw, Courtesy Texas Historical Commission.*

The Remains of Fort St. Louis

Spain learned of France's plans for a North American colony in November 1685, when they captured and interrogated a former La Salle expedition member, Dionisio Thomas—who had defected at Petit-Goâve and become a pirate. The news caused Spanish King Carlos II's Council of War to decree that action was urgently needed "to remove this thorn which had been thrust into the heart of America." Eleven expeditions were eventually launched to find La Salle's colony. On April 22, 1689, Spanish General Alonso de León succeeded in finding the remains of Fort St. Louis. The last few colonists had been killed by the Karankawa just months before.

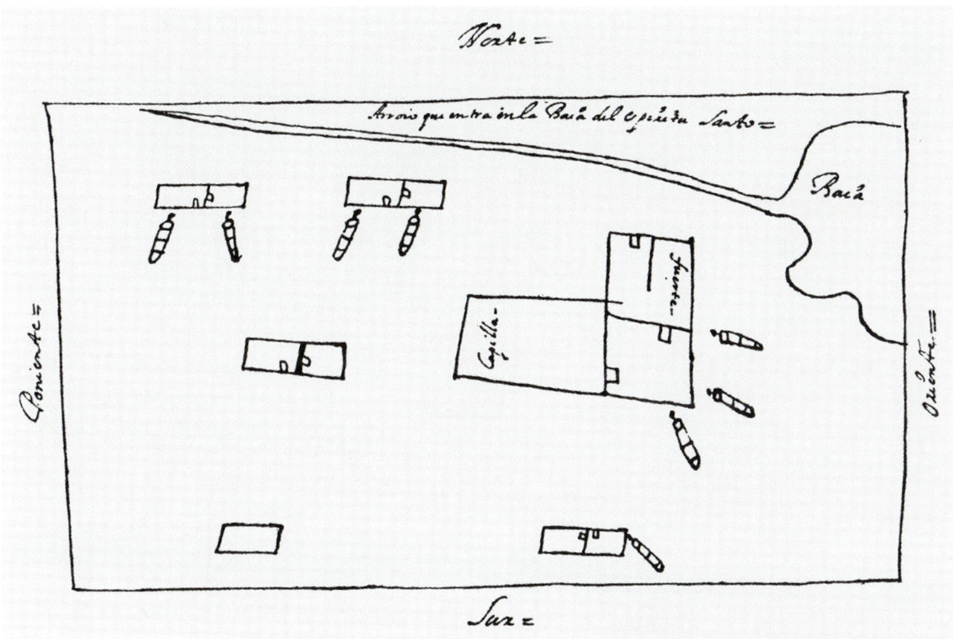

Spanish map of Fort St. Louis, ca. 1689
This map from the Alonso de León expedition shows the settlement's layout, and notes the location of eight iron cannons that guarded the colony. The map also shows the *Fuerte*, a building used as the stronghold by La Salle and the *Capilla*, a small chapel built by the expedition's priests. *Courtesy Yale Collection of Western Americana, Beinecke Rare Book & Manuscript Library.*

Iron cannons in situ
La Salle's eight iron cannons were excavated by Texas Historical Commission archaeologists at Fort St. Louis in September 1996. The cannons were brought to North America aboard *L'Aimable* and off-loaded at the entrance to Matagorda Bay as part of an effort to lighten the vessel as it entered the bay. The ship ultimately ran aground, but the eight cannons were transported to Fort St. Louis. They guarded the settlement until Spanish officer Alonso de León arrived in 1689 and buried them at the site. The cannons lay hidden until a local ranch foreman discovered them in 1996. *Courtesy Texas Historical Commission.*

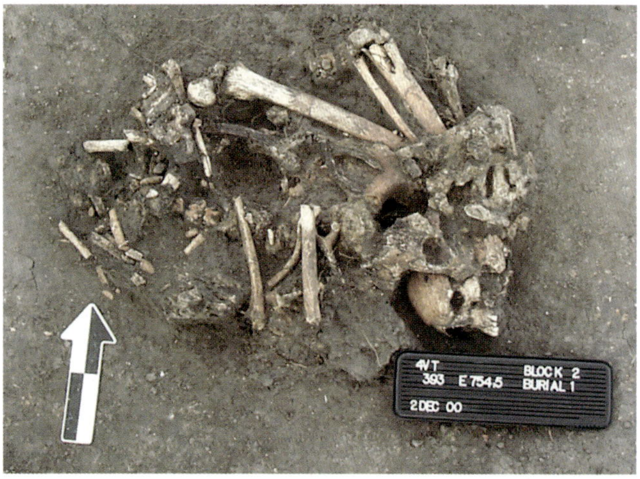

Human remains in situ
When Spaniard Alonso de León arrived at Fort St. Louis in 1689, he found more than the settlement buildings. He encountered the remains of three dead French colonists who had been killed by the Karankawa Indians. The corpses were disarticulated and had been scattered by scavengers, possibly wolves. One of the bodies contained arrows and portions of a dress still clung to the bones. The Spanish recognized this as a woman and identified the other remains as those of a man and a boy. The Spanish soldiers gathered up the remains, buried them, and erected a cross over the grave. *Courtesy Texas Historical Commission.*

Skull of French colonist
Texas Historical Commission archaeologists found the remains of the French colonists in November 2000. The Spanish had buried the disarticulated bodies in a common circular grave located in front of the chapel at Fort St. Louis. Forensic analysis verified three bodies. One was a female between twenty-five and thirty years of age whose head had been struck by a club. Very likely these are the remains of Isabelle Planteaux Talon. This is based on a French interrogation of Jean-Baptiste Talon—a young boy who witnessed and survived the Indian massacre—who saw his mother killed by the Karankawa. Another skeleton was a male (above) of thirty to forty-five years of age, killed by blunt head trauma and a penetrating cranial impact. This was most likely Sieur de La Sablonnière based on other forensic evidence backed by first-person accounts. A juvenile skeleton was also recovered. Forensic and DNA analysis determined the remains to be a male, seven to ten years old. His cause of death could not be determined, and his identity is unknown. *Photograph by H. Gill King, Courtesy Texas Historical Commission.*

Mournful and sad place,
Where gloom alone attends you,
Because sad fortune
Gave you inhabitants a beastly death.
Here I only contemplate
That you are a fatality and a sad example
Of the inconstancy of life
Because the wild and murderous enemy,
So cruel and inhuman,
Discharged his cruelty with a stubborn hand
Against such an innocence,
Not pardoning even the youngest child.

Oh beautiful Frenchwoman
Who walked over fresh roses in these meadows
And with snowy hands touched white lily in brief field
And in beautiful drawing
Put the finishing touches on Greek ladies
Because your ivory [needles]
Adorned the seams with profiles
As deceased as you are,
These forests all together look at you
And, not spoiled in vain,
See themselves through your death, and so misused!

And you cold corpse,
Who at one time showed such vigor,
And now by animals
Eaten, as your remains show,
I contemplate you tenderly,
And you are a living example of unhappiness.
You enjoy eternal glory,
Because you went from this transitory life
To a celestial dwelling,
Going with such a wounded transcended.
Pray to Eternal God)
That he free us from the pains of hell.

This translated version of the poem recorded by Juan Bautista Chapa can be found in William C. Foster, ed., *Texas & Northeastern Mexico, 1630–1690* (Austin: University of Texas Press, 1997): 134–35.

Spanish poem

The first known poem to have been written on Texas soil was composed in 1689 by one of the Spanish officers, Juan Bautista Chapa, about a murdered woman at Fort St. Louis. Historical documents suggest the body was Isabelle Planteaux Talon, one of the few women brought on the expedition.

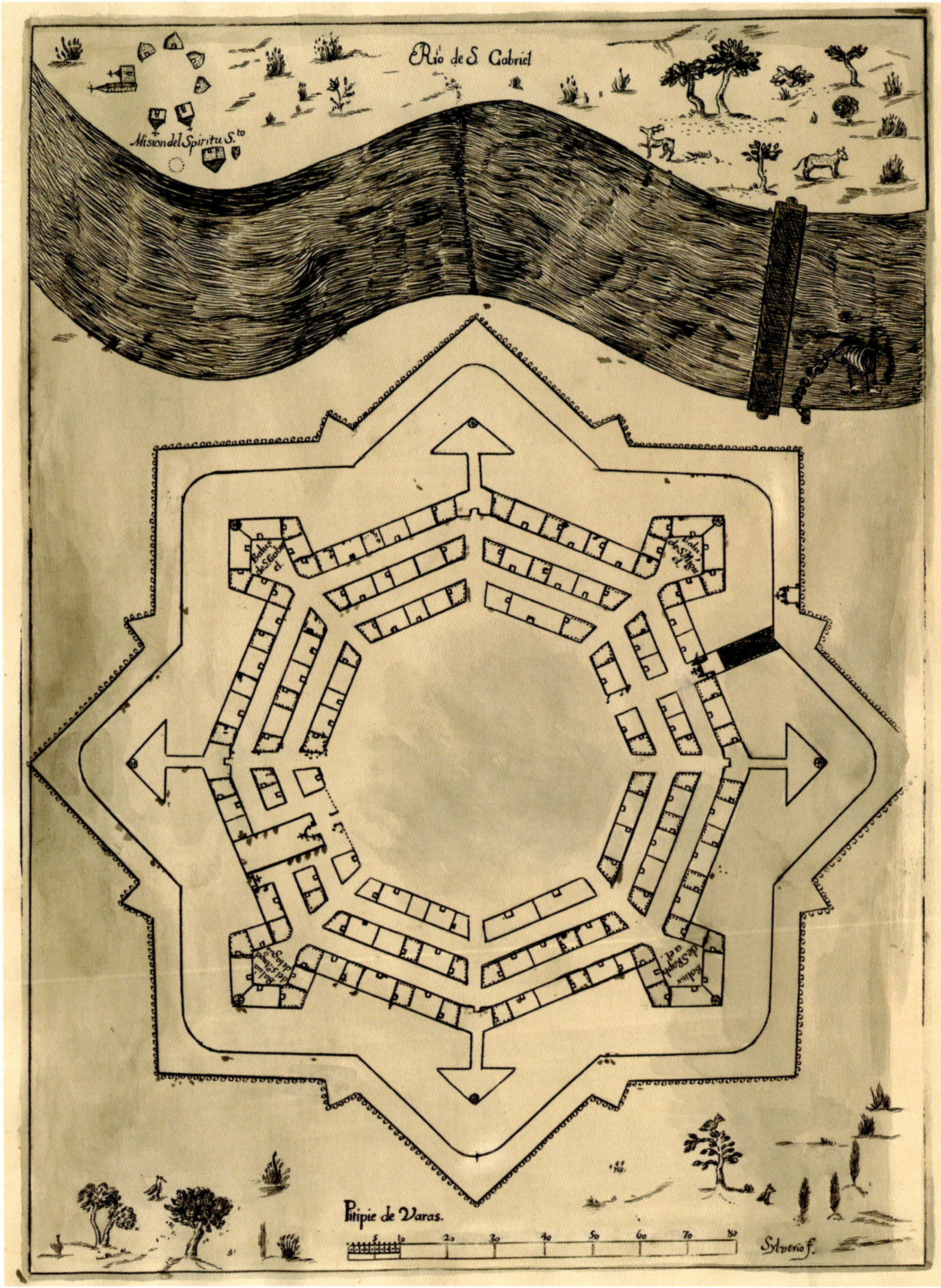

Plan of Presidio La Bahía, ca. 1722
On April 4, 1721, forty soldiers under the command of Captain José Domingo Ramón arrived at the site of Fort St. Louis, preparing to build a Spanish presidio, or fortification, on top of the remains of the French colony. The following year, the Marqués de San Miguel de Aguayo arrived with a larger group of men to begin constructing the presidio. His plan is shown in the drawing. It represented the most complex fortification on the northern frontier of New Spain at that time. The fortification consisted of a stockade with sixteen points in the shape of a star. The elaborate design of the presidio reflects Spanish fears about a possible French return to this part of the Gulf of Mexico. Archaeological excavations by the Texas Historical Commission from 1999 to 2002 unearthed traces of the stockade wall. *Courtesy Bryan (James Perry) Papers, di_08878, The Dolph Briscoe Center for American History, The University of Texas at Austin.*

La Salle brought with him all the supplies he believed he would need — a kit for building a colony in North America.

The Colony Kit

James E. Bruseth

La Belle was not a treasure ship carrying gold, silver, or precious gems—it was a ship of colonization loaded with supplies to support a New World settlement. Before leaving France, four ships were loaded with the cargo La Salle thought he needed. A list of the supplies given by King Louis XIV for the expedition is found in a March 23, 1684, memorandum. In addition to two ships, *Le Joly* and *L'Aimable*, along with crew and soldiers, the memorandum identifies:

- 108,000 pounds of gunpowder
- 32,000 pounds of bullets
- 400 firearms
- 150 swords
- 4 bronze cannons
- 8 iron cannons
- 2,400 cannonballs
- 6 petards of the smallest size
- 300 to 400 grenades
- 50 polearms
- 100 pistols
- 650 pounds of flat and square iron stock
- 2,150 pounds of iron rod stock
- 650 pounds of steel stock
- Blacksmith equipment
- 500 to 600 pounds of tools for carpenters, joiners, wheelwrights, gunsmiths, masons, and rope-makers
- 400 pounds of wrought iron made into crossbars, iron lumps, and angled pieces
- 540 pounds of axes, shovels, hoes, pickaxes, spades, and other tools
- Provisions for the sick
- 2 sets of church furniture[1]

Missing from this list is any mention of trade goods for the Indians. Louis XIV was interested in founding a colony, not engaging in trade with native peoples. However, La Salle and several of the men with him knew that trade with the Indians could be very lucrative. Furs and hides sent back to France could be sold at a handsome profit. For this purpose they personally purchased trade items for commerce with native peoples.

At his Gulf Coast settlement (Fort St. Louis) in the fall of 1685, La Salle loaded *La Belle* with the cargo needed to build a colony at the mouth of the Mississippi River. His goal was to sail *La Belle* to the far end of what he called Bay Saint Louis—today's Matagorda Bay—and then search for a branch of the Mississippi. La Salle's mental image about the geography of the northern Gulf of Mexico is presented in a map hand-drawn by Joutel (on the next page and on page 23). This map, accompanying a manuscript Joutel published in 1713 (see page 20), shows the Mississippi River flowing into the Gulf of Mexico, with one branch projecting far to the west toward an oversized Matagorda Bay. La Salle's goal was to find this branch and sail *La Belle* to the Mississippi, then downstream to a location about 60 miles from the river's mouth to establish his main colony. But he never found the Mississippi and *La Belle* was lost in a storm. For the next three centuries, the ship lay entombed at the bottom of Matagorda Bay, awaiting its modern discovery.[2]

When *La Belle* was excavated during 1996 and 1997, it contained an unexpected, yet unique cargo. Along with supplies and equipment for sailing the seas, *La Belle* contained the resources needed for a New World settlement—a colony kit. Treasure ships laden with gold, silver, and jewels have often been found, but *La Belle* offered an unprecedented opportunity to understand what Frenchmen needed to survive in a remote and unfamiliar frontier. Never before in history had such a cargo been found so intact. *La Belle* was truly a once-in-a-lifetime discovery.

The ship's supplies were packed into eighty-six barrels and eleven boxes. This was only a portion of the original cargo, as only one-third of the vessel's hull remained intact. Nonetheless, when each artifact was individually counted—including thousands of tiny glass trade beads—more than one and a half million objects were recovered.

Accounting for the missing portions of the vessel, as many as three million items may have originally been loaded onto *La Belle*.

Except for trade goods, the cargo largely followed what the king granted to La Salle. Three bronze cannons were found and are part of the original four that were placed deep into the cargo hold to be used as ballast until they would be positioned to defend the new settlement. Placed nearby and also used as ballast were several hundred cannonballs, less than ten percent of what the king had granted. Many barrels of gunpowder, bullets (called lead shot by archaeologists), and birdshot were packed around the cannon balls and in the rear cargo hold. The weight of the gunpowder was calculated to be 21,500 pounds, representing about one-fifth of what was given to La Salle. The bullets weighed 32,000 pounds, nearly identical to what La Salle received. These small lead balls were critical to survival and defense, and were carefully rationed to conserve supplies.

A large quantity of bar stock was recovered and conforms closely to what the king gave La Salle. Square, flat, and rod stock were found, representing about one-quarter of the original supply. Other recovered items include small pieces of rod stock to be made into nails; grinding stones for sharpening tools; brass wire for repairing and making things; muskets for hunting and defense; polearms, grenades, and petards for military actions. These last three objects demonstrate the secret mission of the expedition. They are offensive weapons and would be necessary for attempting to overtake a Spanish fortification. The silver mines of Nueva Viscaya—or northern New Spain (today's Mexico)—were defended by Spanish presidios and other outposts, and to capture Spain's lucrative mines, France would need to attack them.

Other archaeological discoveries tell of the daily life of the colonists, including tableware for dining, brass kettles for cooking, pewter and ceramic plates for serving, glass bottles for wine and spirits, and jars of medicine. Two handsome brass candlestick holders and several candle snuffers—both utterly unessential but nonetheless hauled across the ocean—reveal efforts to maintain French cultural refinements, even in the remote New World frontier. Several excavated artifacts were used for writing, such as pen quill sharpeners, ink wells, brass signets for sealing wax on letters, and even the wax itself.

Thousands of objects were found that related to trade with the Indians. Glass beads and bells were popular with

Map from *Journal historique Du dernier voiage que Monsieur de la Salle à fait dans L'amérique Septentrionale*, ca. 1712
Detail of Joutel's hand-drawn map showing a branch of the Mississippi River flowing west toward an oversized Matagorda Bay. This is where La Salle hoped *La Belle* would access the Mississippi. *Courtesy of the Trustees of the Boston Public Library/Rare Books.*

native peoples, who sewed them onto their clothing and costumes. Finger rings, brass pins, mirrors, axe heads, and knives would have been traded for furs, hides, and other supplies needed by the colonists.

The cargo from *La Belle* offers an opportunity to understand the mindset of La Salle. Much has been written about his mental competence—or possible incompetence. But the artifacts from the shipwreck, especially the items brought to support a colony in the New World, show great planning and extensive knowledge of what was needed for success. La Salle personally oversaw the purchase and loading of supplies onto his ships, and *La Belle*'s cargo is silent testimony to the great explorer's vast experience and his keen knowledge of what he needed to establish a European colony in an unknown and distant land.[3]

Transport and Storage

Barrels were the preferred way to store cargo aboard a ship. They could be rolled for easy transport, and their form fit into the curve of a ship's hold. Barrels could also be watertight to carry water or spirits.

Barrels in situ
La Belle's cargo was placed into barrels and boxes for transportation. Most were unearthed exactly as they were when loaded onto the ship in late 1685. *Courtesy Texas Historical Commission.*

Cooper's bench
Barrels were made by coopers, specialists in making wood containers for liquids. The bench used by one of La Salle's coopers to make the staves for barrels was found in the ship's pump locker, a small compartment that housed the pumps for removing water. *Dimensions 24"l x 7.99"w x 4.17"h*

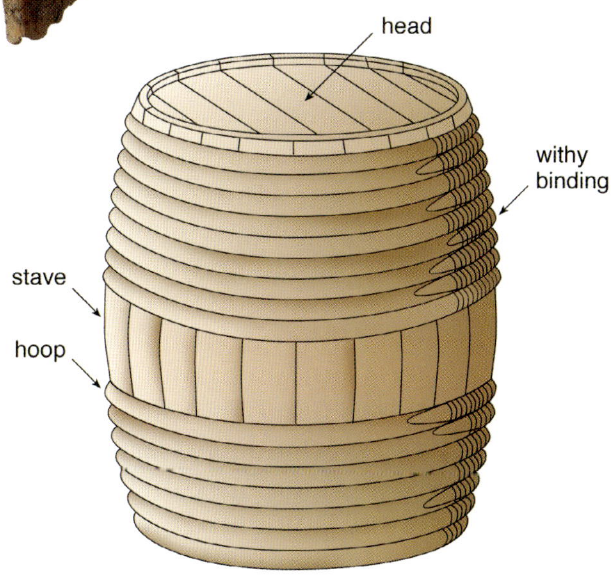

Illustration of barrel construction
Courtesy Texas Historical Commission.

Weapons for Protection and Survival

La Salle's expedition was well stocked with weapons so its members could defend themselves, attack the Spanish, and hunt for food. Bronze and iron cannons in the ship's hold were to guard the colony, while deck cannons and smaller swivel guns protected the ships.

The cargo included two kinds of long arms and several sizes of shot or bullets. One-third of the forty barrels found on *La Belle* held shot; another fourteen contained gunpowder. Because these materials could not be obtained in North America, La Salle knew their importance.

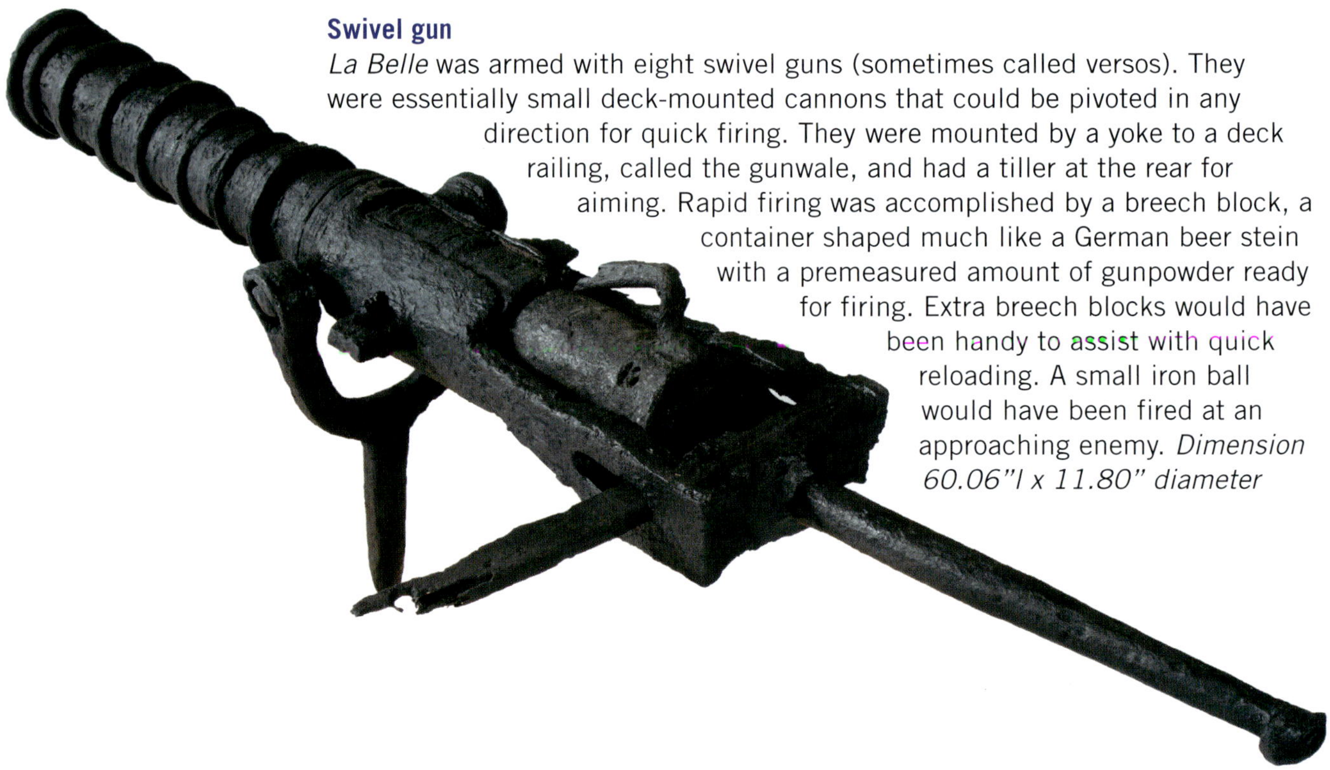

Swivel gun

La Belle was armed with eight swivel guns (sometimes called versos). They were essentially small deck-mounted cannons that could be pivoted in any direction for quick firing. They were mounted by a yoke to a deck railing, called the gunwale, and had a tiller at the rear for aiming. Rapid firing was accomplished by a breech block, a container shaped much like a German beer stein with a premeasured amount of gunpowder ready for firing. Extra breech blocks would have been handy to assist with quick reloading. A small iron ball would have been fired at an approaching enemy. *Dimension 60.06"l x 11.80" diameter*

Bronze cannons in situ
Deep in the main cargo hold, two additional bronze cannons were found. They were identical to the first cannon found on the excavation site, except for markings on the base ring near the breech. Originally King Louis XIV had given four bronze cannons to La Salle, as mentioned in a memorandum signed at Versailles in 1684. The fourth cannon was missing, but a concreted mold from the bottom side of the cannon was found on the port side of the hull, showing that once another cannon, just like the other three, had been there. Its fate is currently unknown. *Courtesy Texas Historical Commission.*

Cannon markings
The first cannon bears the markings "No 4 No 741." At the time of the excavation, archaeologists were uncertain about what the markings represented. The last part, "No 741," might be the weight, but the modern weight was closer to 800 pounds. The "No 4" was a complete mystery. The other cannons' numbers were different: "746# No 84" and "744# No 85."

List of cannons made in Rochefort, France, September 15, 1682

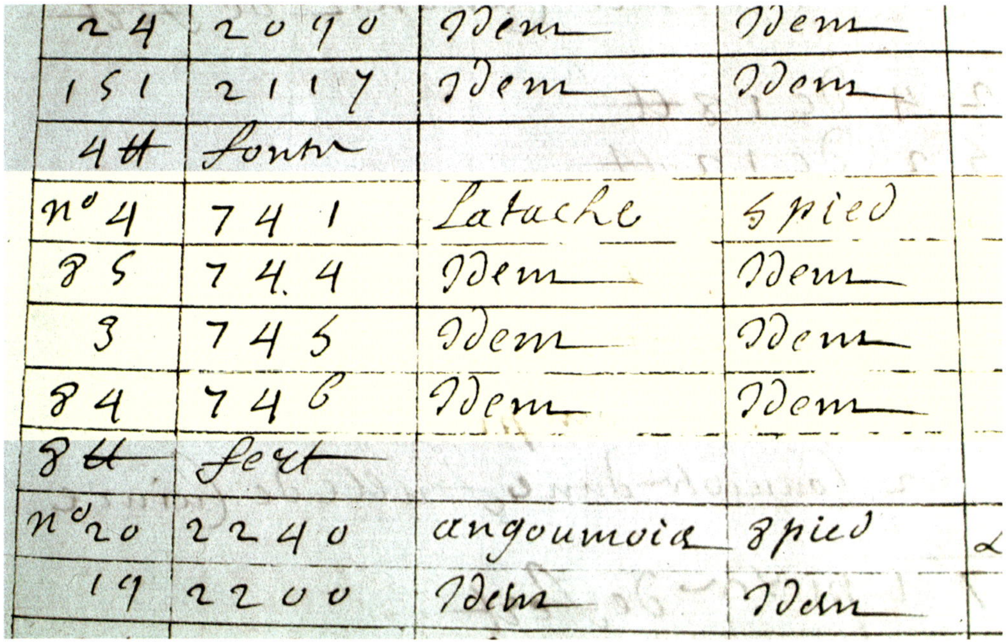

24	2090	Idem	Idem
151	2117	Idem	Idem
4tt	fonte		
no 4	741	Latache	5 pied
85	744	Idem	Idem
3	745	Idem	Idem
84	746	Idem	Idem
8tt	fert		
no 20	2240	angoumois	8 pied
19	2200	Idem	Idem

The clue to unraveling the markings was found in a document in the French Archives at the Port de Rochefort dated September 15, 1682. On one page were entries of four cannons, three with markings identical to *La Belle*'s cannons. The page also identifies what the markings represent. The first part (No 4) is a number assigned to the cannons by the foundry and the other number (No 741) is the weight in French pounds. The document also lists that Latache was the person in charge of the castings and that the cannons were five French feet in length. *Courtesy Archives du Port de Rochefort, Service historique de la Défense, Rochefort, France.*

Cannon balls

La Belle contained various sizes of round shot for the ship's cannons. Nearly four hundred examples were found, mainly deep in the main hold on top of ballast stone. The round shot came in three sizes averaging 1.8 inches, 2.6 inches, and 3 inches. The sizes reflect the different muzzle bores of the cannons La Salle brought, although a large bore could fire shot of smaller sizes. *Dimensions 2.75" diameter*

Fire pot

Nine *pots-au-feu*, or fire pots, were recovered from the lazarette compartment in the stern. These were incendiary weapons that consisted of a ceramic pot (a) containing gunpowder and a grenade (b). A wooden top (c) was placed over the mouth of the pot and fastened with pieces of cloth and string. Wooden fuse holders would have held a fuse that extended from the grenade through the wooden top and to the outside. The fuse on the fire pot could be lit and the vessel thrown at an approaching enemy. The ceramic pot would explode and then the grenade would also blow apart, severely wounding enemy combatants. They would be useful for La Salle on his secret mission to look for the Spanish silver mines of Nueva Vizcaya in anticipation of an invasion. *Overall dimension 7"l x 7"w x 6.73"h*

Petard

Six iron petards (like this example) were packed deep in the bottom of the bow compartment. These were offensive weapons for blowing open the doors of an enemy fortification. Gunpowder would be packed inside and a fuse would be placed into the petards through a small opening near the bottom. Ring handles, near the rim but mostly broken off on the archaeological examples from *La Belle*, would have been used to connect the petards to a long pole and position them at the doorway of an adversary's fort. With the opening of the petard held firmly against the door, the fuse could be lit and the resulting explosion would blow open the door to allow entry into the building. The petards from *La Belle* reflect weapons brought by La Salle in the event he needed to breach a Spanish fortification, quite possibly as part of his investigation of Spanish silver mines. *Dimension 9.05"l x 9.64"w x 10.62"h*

Polearms

Polearms were weapons commonly used in the Middle Ages, but were declining in use by La Salle's time. Seven examples were found on *La Belle*, two of which are shown here. Depending on their style they would have had different names. The upper specimen is called a halberd, and the lower specimen is a partisan. Halberds have a pike-like spear point on the end for attacking a man on horseback. The hook is for grabbing the enemy and pulling him from the horse. It also has an axe-like blade for cleaving the dismounted man's armor. The partisan's function was more for cutting and twisting into a mounted opponent. The presence of these weapons on *La Belle* is puzzling, as no horses were brought with the expedition. They might also signify military rank among the soldiers. *Dimensions Halberd 23.26"l x 4.48"w x 1.49"h; Partisan 28.50"l x 4.76"w x 1.49"h*

Lead shot in situ
Nearly 120,000 lead shot were found, representing the bullets La Salle's men used in their firearms. Most were packed into twenty-seven barrels deep in the main cargo hold (above). They were located directly on top of the ship's ballast and were themselves acting as ballast. The shot barrels contained lead balls of varying sizes, ranging from one-half inch to one inch in diameter. *Courtesy Texas Historical Commission.*

Longarms in situ
The longarms were of two types that investigators have called patterns. Pattern A (see pages 76–77) was a buccaneer-style gun for long-range shooting. Pattern B was a regulation military musket, then referred to as a *fusil ordinaire*. Firearm manufacture at this time was not standardized, and barrel diameters varied slightly. Therefore each gun might use lead shot of a slightly different diameter. It was not critical to size the bullet exactly to the bore of the gun. Joutel tells of firing bullets cut in half to conserve them. In another case, he mentions three bullets being fired from a single musket shot. Standardization of French firearms did not come for another thirty years, when barrel diameters became uniform. *Courtesy Texas Historical Commission.*

Pattern A longarm reconstruction
Reconstruction by Conservation Research Laboratory, Texas A&M University, College Station; Dimension 70.8"l x 2.24"w x 5.15"h

Sun King medallion
Several of the firearms displayed the sun symbol of King Louis XIV embedded into the stock, signifying that the weapons were part of the king's arms. *Dimension .98"l x .98"w x .23"h*

Gunpowder cartridge
Gunpowder for firing the colonists' guns was sometimes premeasured and stored in small cartridges, often called apostles. They would have been attached to a shoulder belt, called a bandolier. The wooden containers consisted of a long wood tube with a wood top. A piece of string or twine would be tied to the top and strung through loops in the tube. This allowed the top to be quickly removed, and the correct amount of gunpowder to be poured into the gun barrel. The string would keep the top hanging nearby so as not to lose it. *Dimension 3.93"l x 1.37"w x 1.41"h*

Gunflints

Stone gunflints were used to ignite gunpowder in the colonists' guns. Three hundred and fifty-eight flints were found in various parts of the ship. They would have been held in the jaws of the gun cock (below) with a piece of cloth or leather. When the cock was released it would strike the frizzen, an L-shaped metal arm, and create sparks to ignite gunpowder in the pan. The ignited powder would burn through a small hole in the barrel of the gun, igniting a powder charge in the barrel and propelling a lead bullet. *Dimensions of gunflint 1"l x 1"w x .30"h*

Pair of drumsticks
Drumsticks were used with a drum by soldiers for keeping a steady pace during marches and to time the loading and firing of guns. *Dimensions 15.82"l x .98" diameter*

Brass powder flask
Another method for measuring the correct amount of gunpowder needed for a charge was a powder flask. The photograph shows a brass example with a metal arm for premeasuring gunpowder. A colonist would put his finger over the tip of the flask, turn it upside down, and slide the brass arm to hold the remaining gunpowder inside the body of the flask. Once the right amount of gunpowder was measured, the finger could be removed and the flask poured into the gun barrel. *Dimension 7.51"l x 4.01"w x 2.51"h*

Household Items

La Belle's exceptionally well-preserved contents give us insight into what the French thought essential to establishing a colony in the Americas. These included the necessities of daily life: ceramic containers, pewter plates and bowls, bottles, cooking pots and utensils, candlesticks, and writing tools.

Ceramic containers

La Belle contained several intact or partially complete ceramic vessels. Many were for serving and eating food, such as a pitcher for wine (below, left) and a plate for eating (bottom). Others were tall cylindrical jars that contained medicines (below, right). Many of the ceramics came from the community of La Chapelle des Pots near La Rochelle. Other vessels came from Nevers, Rouen, Beauvaisis, and Sadirac—all areas of France specializing in particular ceramic wares. *Dimension Plate 7.08"l x 3.30"w x 1.2"h; Wine pitcher 7.79"h x 5.25" diameter; Medicine jar 6.16"h x 3.70" diameter*

Pewter plates
The most common dinnerware found on *La Belle* was pewter plates, but some pewter bowls and porringers—small cups for eating porridge or other similar food—were also recovered. In the main hold of the ship, a stack of pewter plates was found that had originally been inside a wooden chest, but the chest had largely deteriorated. *Dimensions 9" diameter on average*

Detail of owner's mark
Many of the plates had the initials "LG" stamped on their undersides, probably the initials of Sieur Le Gros, one of the upper class men La Salle brought with him.

On Easter Day of 1685, Le Gros stepped on a rattlesnake that bit him above the ankle. Joutel writes, "We carefully tended to him but, after much suffering . . . [his] leg was still very swollen. The surgeon told him that gangrene threatened to set in and that he could find no remedy other than cutting off the leg. . . When everything was prepared for the operation, his leg was cut off. This happened on the 27th of August [1685]. The amputation was made very close to the knee, and a fever overtook the patient. He lasted only two more days and died the 30th."

Onion bottle

Fifteen glass bottles of two types were found onboard. Onion bottles are named for their bulbous shapes. This bottle would have had a cork stopper and might have contained wine.

Joutel tells us that while *La Belle* lay anchored waiting for La Salle in 1686, "The ship's master took possession of the wine and filled his gullet well indeed." *Dimension 5.19"l x 5.19"w x 7.75"h*

Case bottle

A case bottle has a square body shape made from blowing the glass into a square wooden mold. This allowed it to be stored in a wood case divided into small compartments, each big enough to hold one bottle. The examples from *La Belle* also had pewter screw stops made by applying a screw base to the still soft, partially molten, glass top. This type of bottle would have held alcohol such as brandy. *Dimension 9.0"l x 2.5"w x 2.5"h*

Wooden spoon

Used for preparing and serving food, wooden spoons were a necessary tool on board ship and within the colony. *Dimensions 5.98"l x 2.51"w x .98"h*

Brass fork

High-status passengers, such as priests, would dine at the captain's table in the stern cabin. They would be expected to bring their own plates and eating utensils. Other passengers would eat on deck. *Dimension 6.73"l x .98"w x .74"h*

Wooden scoop

Wooden scoops of this shape were used to transfer dry food stores, such as flour or corn. *Dimension 18.30"l x 3.93"w x 2.36"h*

Brass colander
Dimension 10"l x 10"w x 3.26"h

Brass soup ladle
Dimensions 19.76"l x 4.76"w x 3.50"h

Brass cooking kettle
Dimension 13.74"l x 13.74"w x 9.25"h

Brass candlesticks
Some finer objects were among the cargo, such as these candlesticks. La Salle was accompanied by several wealthy volunteers who were seeking fortunes in North America. They brought with them items that reflected their elegant lifestyles in France. *Dimension 4.72"l x 4.72"w x 6.25"h*

Buttons

Pewter buttons were used as fasteners on soldiers' clothing.

Dimension .50"l x .50"w x .74"h

Red cloth

This red piece of cloth, perhaps from a cape or uniform, was a rare find. Cloth does not typically survive on shipwrecks as it deteriorates too quickly.

Dimension 4.75"l x 1.62"w x .11"h

Thimble

Thimbles were a standard tool in any sewing kit.

Dimension .55"l x .75" diameter

Crucifix

This Roman Catholic crucifix is made of wood with the figure of Christ in brass and would have been part of a rosary, a string of prayer beads. At the bottom are the remains of a skull over crossbones representing the remains of Adam, who brought sin into the world. La Salle brought six Catholic priests with him. Three were from the Récollet Franciscan order and three from the Sulpician order. Most of La Salle's colonists were Catholic, although a few may have been Huguenots, members of the Protestant Reformed Church of France. *Dimension 2.51"l x 1.49"w x 5"h*

Quill pen

Writing instruments were recovered from both the main and aft cargo holds. Among them was a small knife for sharpening quill pens. *Dimension 4.76"l x .55" diameter*

Inkwell
This inkwell brought by the expedition would have contained ink in liquid or cake form. *Dimension 2"l x 2"w x 1.73"h*

Brass signet ring
Once a letter or other written document was finished, it would be folded, and sealed with wax. A stamp would be applied to the liquid wax using a signet brass ring with a decorative insignia on one side. *Dimension .74"l x .51"w x .98"h*

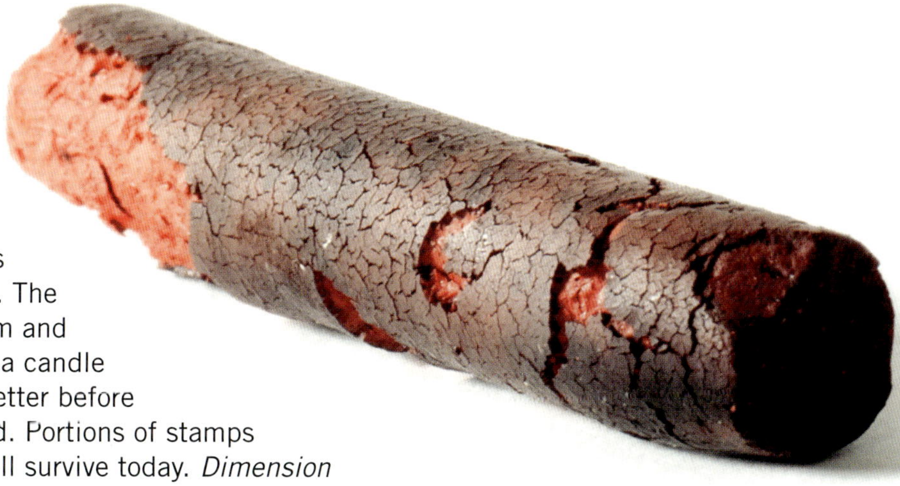

Sealing wax
The red wax for sealing letters and other documents was found in the main hold. The wax was in a cylindrical form and would have been heated by a candle and dripped onto a folded letter before the brass stamp was applied. Portions of stamps that once were on letters still survive today. *Dimension 3.66"l x .48" diameter*

Tools To Build and Sustain a Colony

The settlers brought with them the tools they needed to establish and maintain a new colony. The expedition carried harvesting utensils, carpentry tools, nails, spikes, grinding stones, brass wire, rope, and iron stock to make additional metal tools.

Reaping hook
The reaping hook was an effective tool for cutting grass or crops. *Dimension 15.31"l x 5.5"w x 1.31"h*

Ruler
This ruler would have been an important tool in building the structures at Fort St. Louis. *Dimension 12.83"l x .9"w x .9"h*

Draw knife
The colony's cooper, or barrel maker, would have used a draw knife for smoothing wooden planks and boards. *Dimension 24.25"l x 3.14"w x 2.75"h*

Sharpening stone
Handheld abrasive stones, or hones, were used for sharpening knives and other hand tools quickly.
Dimension 11.49"l x 1.81"w x .74"h

Quern stone
Hand mills were used to grind grain. The mill had two stones, an upper stone called a handstone, and a lower stationary bedstone called a quern stone. The top stone would have had a handle to rotate it, grinding the grain between the upper and lower stones.
Dimension 16.14"l x 16.14"w x 3.58"h

Brass wire

Two large coils of brass wire were found in the aft cargo hold. They were so perfectly preserved that they could have been mistaken for contemporary wire if not found deep inside the shipwreck. The coils were about two feet in diameter and made up of thirty-two smaller coils of differing diameter wire. Wire would have been a multipurpose commodity that could be used to tie things together, make straight pins, connect fencing to poles, and trade with the Indians. *Dimension 21.96"l x 21.96"w x 1.96"h*

Rope

One of the extraordinary aspects of *La Belle* was the preservation of rope, primarily made from hemp. Rope rarely preserves on shipwrecks in the quantity found on *La Belle*. A very large coil of hawser, or anchor rope, was found in the bow with a human skeleton lying in the center (see page 102). Extra rope was stored below deck in the bow compartment until needed. Coils of rope were found in the aft cargo hold, and were part of the supplies brought for the colony. Fragments of other rope were found across the wreck, most associated with the rigging. As the masts and sails deteriorated and fell into the water, pieces became entombed in the wreck and were preserved by the bay sediments. *Dimension 33.46"l x 22.83"w x 5.51"h*

Iron stock

La Salle brought a large quantity of iron stock for the expedition, consisting of blanks used for making nails (right), and flat and round stock more than eight feet long for producing tools and other objects (left).

La Salle also brought two blacksmiths named Jean Leuraud and Jacques Jean. Leuraud was thirty and Jean was sixty-five—one of the oldest members of the expedition. Blacksmiths were critical to the expedition, enabling new tools to be made and old ones to be fixed. The importance of the iron stock is seen in a letter exchanged between La Salle and Captain Beaujeu, who had orders to bring *Le Joly* to the Gulf of Mexico, unload any supplies and colonists, and sail back to France. *Le Joly* carried the expedition's only iron stock that remained after the wrecking of *L'Aimable*, the large supply ship. La Salle asked that the iron stock on *Le Joly* be off-loaded and brought to La Salle before the ship sailed back to France. At first Beaujeu resisted, saying the iron was deep in the cargo hold and that unloading it while anchored off the coast would be too risky, possibly resulting in the loss of the ship. La Salle persisted, saying his colony could not be successful without the stock. Ultimately, Beaujeu relented and found a way to remove the iron and send it to La Salle. The iron rod and bar stock pictured are some of the materials removed from *Le Joly* and given to La Salle. *Dimension Iron stock (right) 4.37"l x .31"w x .18"h average; Bar stock (left) 65.06"l x 2.75"w x .78"h*

The excavation of La Belle *required the building of a steel cofferdam and water pumps to keep the work area dry.*

Discovery, Excavation, and Preservation

JAMES E. BRUSETH *and* TONI S. TURNER

For three centuries, the ship—and La Salle's dreams of conquest and colonization—lay entombed in a watery grave at the bottom of Matagorda Bay, Texas. Guided by seventeenth-century Spanish maps and the expedition journal of Henri Joutel, historians spent one hundred and fifty years speculating about the location of the lost ship. The Texas Historical Commission's (THC) initial quest in the 1970s to find *La Belle* ended without success, but in 1995 technology and good fortune yielded a remarkable discovery. Following a magnetometer signal, divers examined the source and found a magnificent bronze cannon lying on the bottom of the bay. Other artifacts obtained during initial testing of the wreck were also French in origin.[1]

Archival sources had indicated that *La Belle* would be a small ship, measuring 54 feet in length and 15 feet in width. Divers reported that the outline of a hull of the correct size could be traced in the silts of the bay bottom. They also observed barrels and storage boxes in the hull with contents still inside, so a significant portion of the cargo appeared to be intact.

The bronze cannon was raised from the water a few days later and bore an inscription: "*Le Comte de Vermandois*." Vermandois was the Admiral of France from 1669 to 1683, thus dating the wreck to the correct time frame. These discoveries provided incontrovertible proof that *La Belle* had at last been found. The buried ship was ready to reveal its secrets to the world.

With the vessel's identity confirmed, excavation was urgently needed. The fact that *La Belle* still existed in 1995—adjacent to the Intracoastal Waterway canal system and in

Bronze cannon, 1995 Texas Historical Commission archaeologists examine a bronze cannon recovered from the wreck. The bronze cannon provided incontrovertible proof that *La Belle* had been found. *Courtesy Texas Historical Commission.*

Building the cofferdam walls, 1996
A large mechanical vibrator was used to drive the sheets of steel piling into the bay bottom. The walls would allow archaeologists to excavate as if *La Belle* were on dry land. *Courtesy Texas Historical Commission.*

Extra strength, 1996
Sand was dumped between two rows of sheet piling to form the wall of the cofferdam. The extra strength provided by the sand wall would protect the excavation site from storms. *Courtesy Texas Historical Commission.*

the path of extensive oil exploration—demanded immediate protection and investigation. The shipwreck also lay in a remote area along the southern shore of the bay, where it was vulnerable to the exploitation of treasure hunters.

The THC decided to conduct a full recovery in a single season. To ensure the highest standards of scientific excavation, including the precise recording of artifacts and the recovery of fragile remains, a bold and innovative methodology was proposed. A steel cofferdam would be constructed around the wreck, allowing seawater to be removed and the excavation to proceed as if *La Belle* lay on dry land. It would be the first time a dewatered cofferdam excavation had been conducted in the Western Hemisphere, and the risk and expense were enormous.

During the early summer of 1996 construction began on the cofferdam. The plans called for an octagonal-shaped structure, measuring 178 feet in length and 131 feet in width. The wall of the cofferdam would actually consist of two rows of steel sheet piling, 33 feet apart. Steel sheet piling was specially manufactured in Pennsylvania and transported to Matagorda Bay for the construction. A large crane positioned the pilings, and they were driven forty feet into the bay floor to keep water from seeping inside. Then sand was placed between the two rows of sheet piling to form the overall wall of the dam. This massive structure was needed to provide the strength to withstand storms—like the one that sank *La Belle* more than three centuries earlier.

A steel roof was placed over the interior of the cofferdam to protect the excavation site from sun and inclement weather. Once artifacts were uncovered, they had to be kept wet to prevent them from drying out.

The cofferdam was completed in September, and the removal of the water began. The project engineers stated that the cofferdam would leak. They thought four sump pumps could remove any water that leaked in, but the pumps would have to run constantly, twenty-four hours a day. They also warned that there was a small chance that the water leakage would be so great that pumps could not keep up with it. In this case, the cofferdam would be a catastrophic failure.

As the pumps droned on, the water inside the cofferdam slowly began to recede. After a few days, the bottom of Matagorda Bay was exposed for the first time in untold millennia. Sitting on the bay floor were artifacts from *La Belle*. Soon it was clear that the pumps could keep up with the minimal leakage of water through the walls.

The gamble to build a huge steel cofferdam and pump out the water paid off. It allowed archaeologists to excavate *La Belle* as if it were on dry land. Many of the daily crew activities took place on the wall of the cofferdam, including screening of all the sediments that had encapsulated the wreck after sinking. Over the ensuing seven months, more than 1.6 million artifacts were unearthed, ranking *La Belle* as one of the most important shipwrecks ever discovered in North America.

A large crane allowed heavier artifacts to be lifted from inside the cofferdam to the wall for transport by boat back to the project headquarters in Palacios, Texas, 1 hour and 15 minutes away. The crane also lifted heavy buckets of sediment for screening.

One of the more important activities that took place on the wall of the cofferdam was the generation of electricity by two diesel engines. Many of the systems on the cofferdam, such as the sump pumps and the project computers, required a continuous electrical supply.

Archaeologists uncovered bronze cannons, glass beads, bells, pottery, tools, weapons, and even the skeleton of a crew

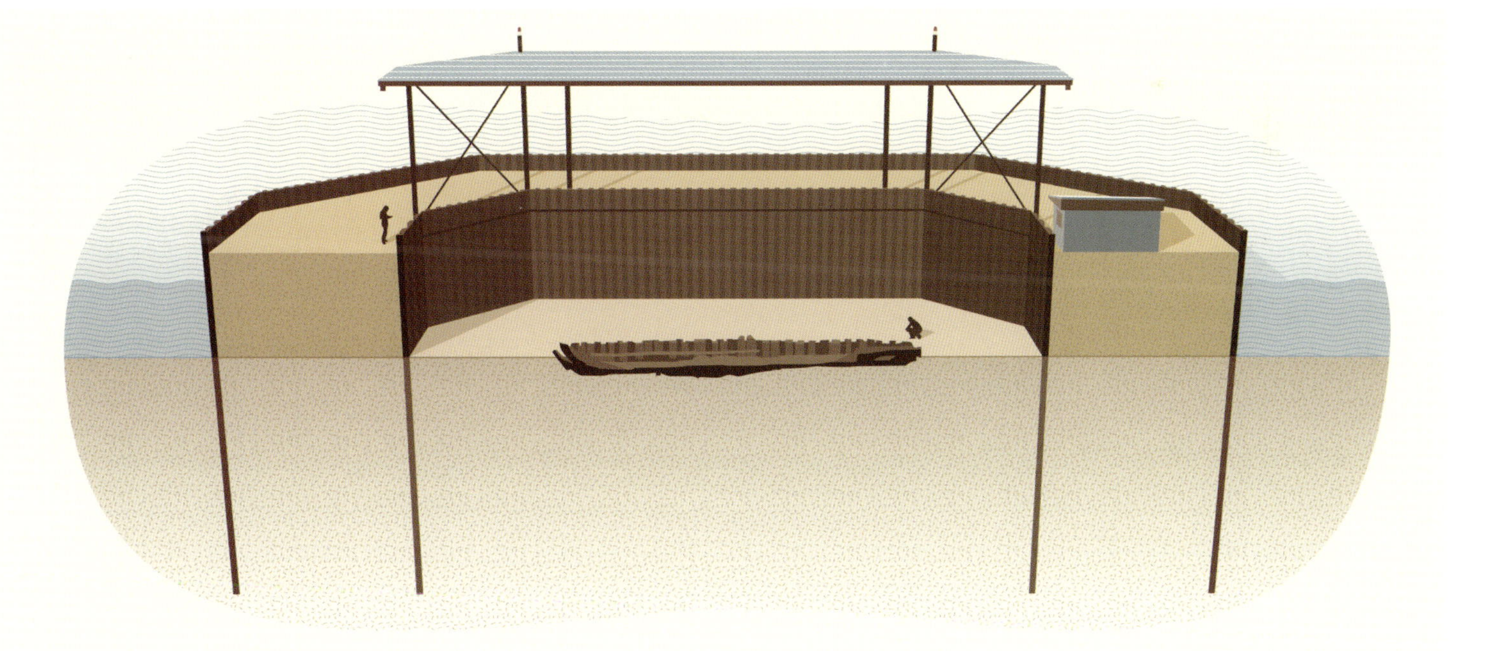

Cut-away illustration of the completed cofferdam
The completed cofferdam included a steel roof to shield workers and artifacts from the elements.

member. Analysis of the artifacts told a remarkable story. To the amazement of the archaeologists and conservation experts, preservation in the ship was truly extraordinary, due to the anaerobic environment created by the bay sediments that encapsulated the wreck. Excavations produced virtually intact remnants of fabric, rope, basketry, yarn, bones, and insects. Caches of muskets, lead shot, cannonballs, and armaments demonstrated that the colonists expected to face dangerous conditions in this unknown land. Human skeletal remains found in the ship's bow gave silent testimony to the final days of a man who had found death in the New World instead of a new life. Each day, more discoveries opened windows into the past, revealing an intimate glimpse of daily life aboard a sailing ship three centuries ago.

An international team of historians and archivists pored over documents in France, Spain, and the United States, yielding new information related to the ship's purchase, construction, cargo, and crew. These documents also confirmed that *La Belle* was an official vessel of Louis XIV's fleet and was therefore French property (see Foreword).

All of the artifacts from *La Belle*, including the hull, were taken to the Conservation Research Laboratory at Texas A&M University's Riverside Campus in College Station, Texas. The lab specializes in the preservation of objects from a marine environment, and has been a leader in developing many of the methods for the treatment of shipwreck artifacts.

Seven museums along the central Texas coast comprise what is called the La Salle Odyssey and tell the story of La Salle's expedition in Texas. The museums are the Corpus Christi Museum of Science and History (which also stores *La Belle* artifacts not on display), the Texas Maritime Museum in Rockport, the Calhoun County Museum in Port Lavaca, the Museum of the Coastal Bend in Victoria, the Texana Museum in Edna, the City by the Sea Museum in Palacios, and the Matagorda County Museum in Bay City. Using artifacts from *La Belle*, each museum tells a different part of the broader story of France's ill-fated attempt to establish a colony along the northern Gulf of Mexico.

Finding *La Belle*

Archaeologists knew that *La Belle* was somewhere in Matagorda Bay but did not know its exact location. Positioning systems and magnetometers paired with archival maps helped marine archaeologists find the shipwreck.

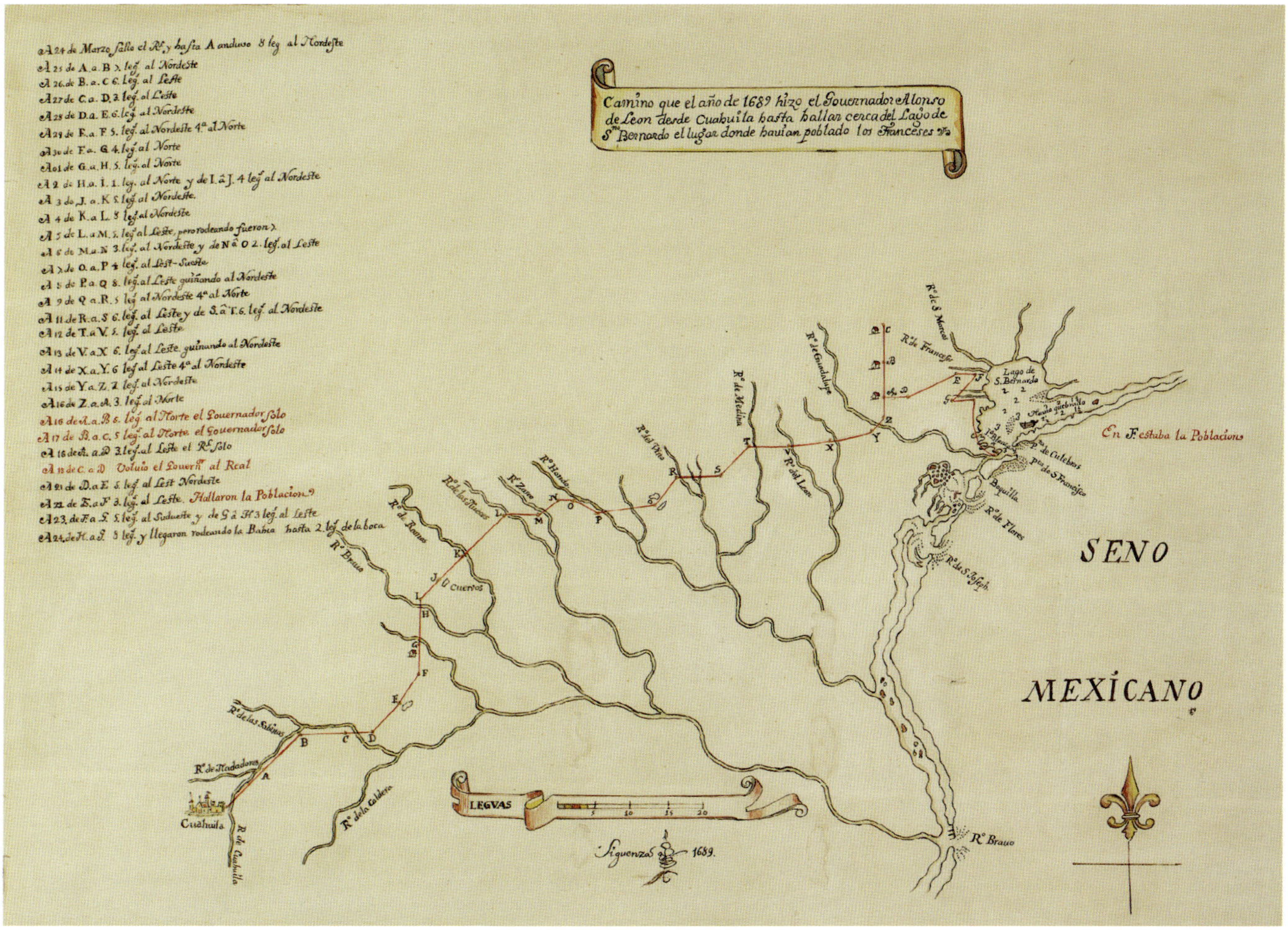

Map of Matagorda Bay by Carlos Sigüenza y Góngora, ca. 1690s
Spanish searches for *La Belle* resulted in a map of Matagorda Bay by Carlos Sigüenza y Góngora based on sketches from Alonso de León's 1689 quest to find Fort St. Louis. The red line on the map shows the route of de León's expedition from Coahuila, Mexico, to Lago de Santo Bernardo, or today's Matagorda Bay. *Courtesy Bryan (James Perry) Papers, di_03214, The Dolph Briscoe Center for American History, The University of Texas at Austin.*

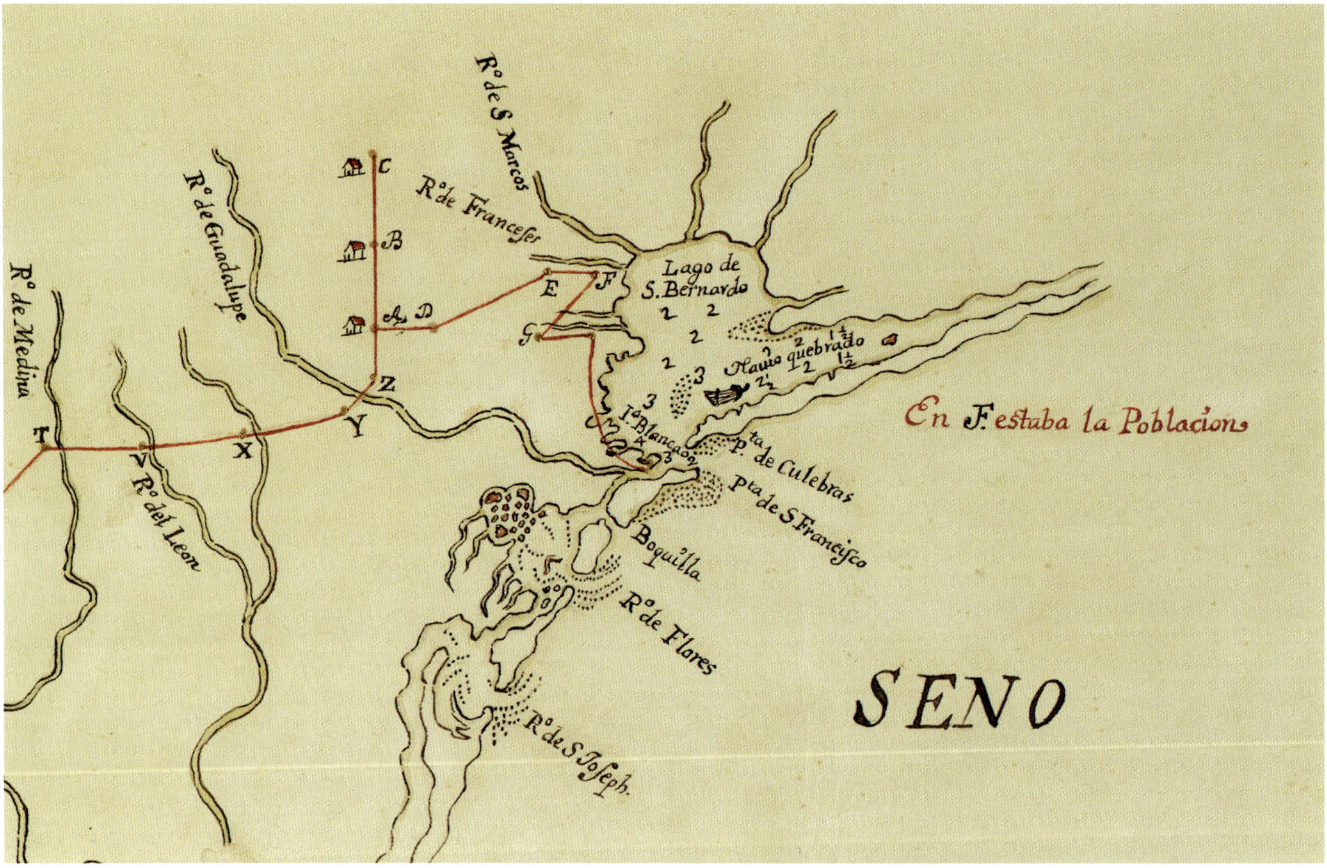

Detail of Map of Matagorda Bay

This depicts the bay and the location of Fort St. Louis (represented by the letter F) and *Navío quebrado* (Spanish for "broken ship") denoting the wreck of *La Belle*. The location of *La Belle* on the map is based on Juan Enríquez Barroto's 1687 maritime search for La Salle's colony. Barroto was the pilot of the *Nuestra Señora del Rosario*, one of two shallow-draft *piraguas* (flat-bottomed boat well-suited to rivers) sent to look for La Salle. His expedition failed to find Fort St. Louis, but it did locate *La Belle*, wrecked in the bay. He described it as "inside a bay on the windward shore, . . . 3 fleurs-de-lis on her poop." Texas Historical Commission archaeologists used this map to determine where to look for the wreck. *Courtesy Bryan (James Perry) Papers, di_03214, The Dolph Briscoe Center for American History, The University of Texas at Austin.*

Discovery of a Cannon

In 1995, the Texas Historical Commission surveyed Matagorda Bay for areas of high magnetism, indicators of potential shipwrecks. Scuba divers were prepared to investigate each of the thirty-nine possibilities, but the first dive of the first day yielded amazing results.

Bronze cannon
When Texas Historical Commission divers identified this bronze cannon buried in the bay sediments of Matagorda Bay, they knew they had made a great find. Cannons typically indicate old wrecks. A few days later, the cannon was raised from the bottom of the bay and cleaning revealed a French inscription "Le Comte de Vermandois." *Dimensions 72"l x 14"w x 25.98"h*

Admiral of the French Fleet (*below*)
Research found that the count (*comte*) was the child of Louise de la Vallière, a mistress of the French King Louis XIV. Her relationship with the king began around 1661 and a son named Louis de Bourbon was born in 1667. The king legitimized the birth of the child in 1669 by naming him Le Comte de Vermandois and appointing him admiral of the French fleet. The cannon confirmed that *La Belle* had been found, after lying in a watery grave for 309 years. *Courtesy Texas Historical Commission.*

Archaeologists at Work

A crew of sixteen to twenty archaeologists traveled fifteen miles each way from Palacios, Texas, to the cofferdam by boat to carefully unearth *La Belle* and its cargo.

On the dig, 1996
Sometimes archaeologists lay on pick boards suspended over the wreck to excavate artifacts. *Courtesy Texas Historical Commission.*

Mapping the site, 1996
The cofferdam allowed the archaeologists to excavate *La Belle* with the same care and precision as a land-based investigation would offer. Detailed mapping of artifacts took place as the wreck deposits were exposed. *Courtesy Texas Historical Commission.*

Screening, 1997
All of the sediment surrounding larger artifacts was screened on the cofferdam wall. Thousands of very small artifacts were recovered through this meticulous process. *Courtesy © 1997 Kay Chernush.*

Site Excavation Grid

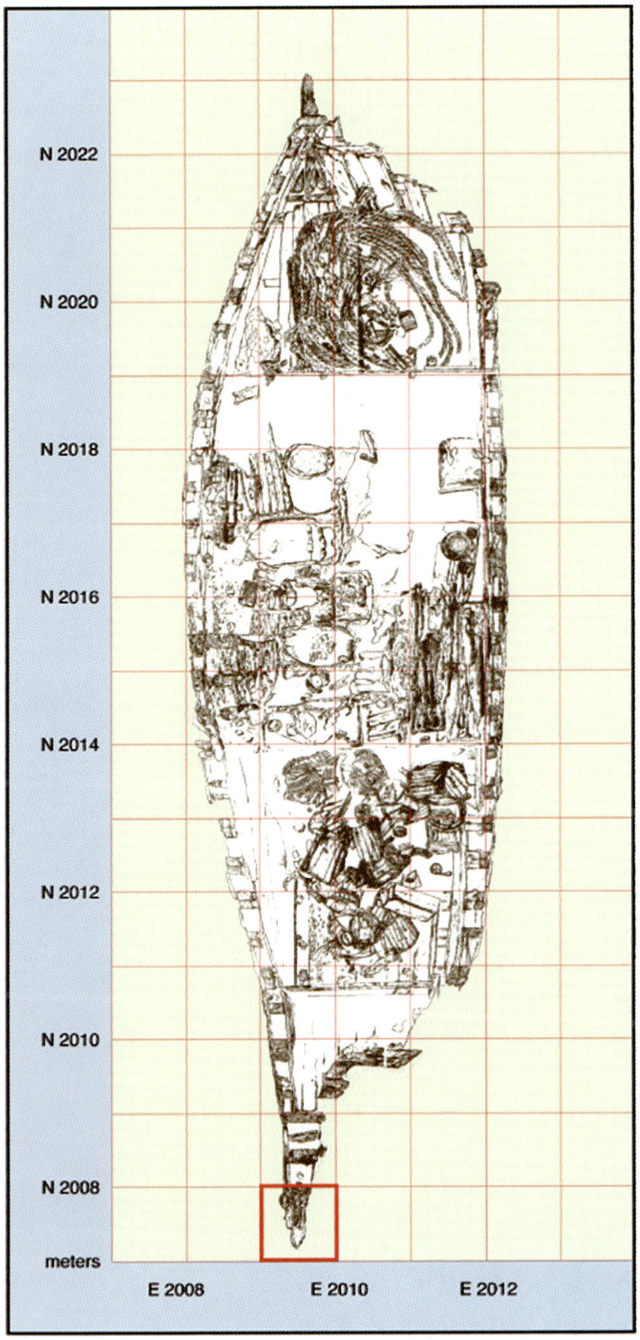

A site grid was established to keep track of the locations of all of the recovered artifacts. The grid consisted of 1-meter squares superimposed over the site. Each square was labeled by its north and east location. For instance, grid unit North 2007 and East 2009 would be the square at the end of the vessel that included the stern of the ship (see the square denoted with a red outline). Excavation took place within each square and 10 cm (or 4 inch) levels were dug. All artifacts were carefully mapped by hand and also by an electronic data station—an instrument that used a laser to record precise readings of distance and depth.

Excavation Grid, 2004
Courtesy Texas Historical Commission.

Skeleton in the Ship

During the excavation of *La Belle*, a skeleton was discovered deep inside the ship's bow. It lay on top of a large coil of anchor rope, with other artifacts nearby.

Skeleton in situ

Forensic anthropological studies indicated that the remains represented a European male in his late thirties to early forties. He was about five feet five inches tall and had suffered several traumas and medical disorders. He had been struck on the right side of his face with sufficient force to break his nose. He had a herniated disk and other lower back problems that would have caused him to walk with a painful limp. His teeth contained severe cavities and he had lost several of them. Infection related to this tooth loss caused part of his jaw to be eaten away. Wear patterns on his front teeth showed that they had been used as tools to grasp some type of fibrous material. *Photograph by Robert Clark, Courtesy Texas Historical Commission.*

Surrounding the skeleton
Several artifacts were found around the skeleton including a water barrel, a pewter porringer (cup), and parts of several shoes and a shoe last (a mold for forming leather into a shoe). The cup was inscribed "C Barange," possibly the deceased crew member's name. Several of the crew died of thirst while onboard *La Belle* waiting for La Salle to return. *Dimensions Water barrel 10"l x 10"w x 9"h; Porringer 5.51"l x 3.74"w x .94"h; Shoe last 9.01"l x 4.01"w x 5.98"h*

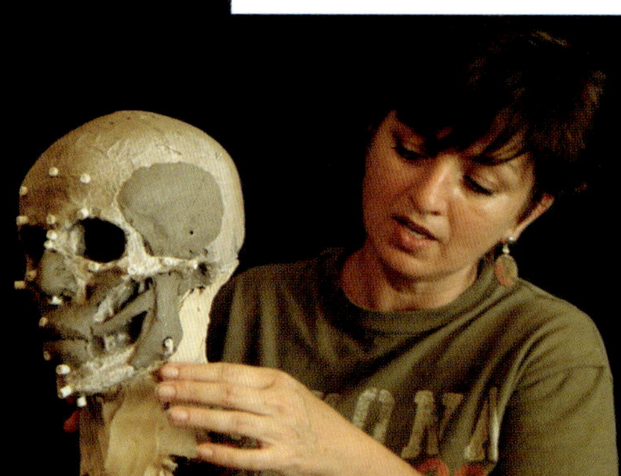

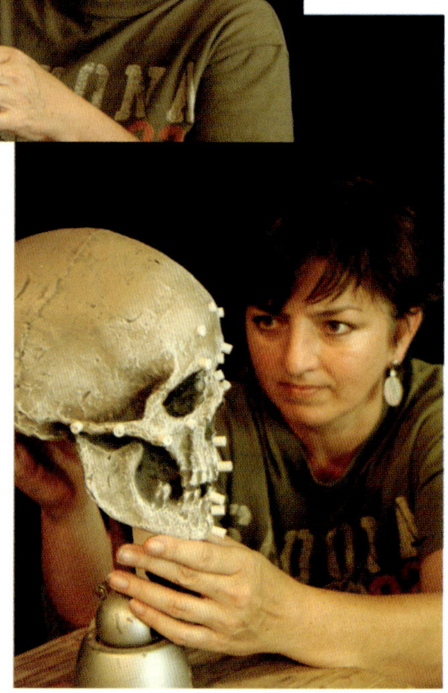

Reconstructed face

Forensic sculptor Amanda Danning reconstructed the face of the skeleton found on *La Belle*. After reviewing the physical anthropologist's report, she commenced work on the skull by adding appropriate muscles to the replica skull. Next, she added soft tissue depth markers appropriate for someone of this person's gender and body type in order to help fill out the face in areas where there was no musculature representation. Danning studied the nuances of the skull in order to determine unique facial characteristics, including wrinkles and scars. *Courtesy Amanda Danning.*

Remains of the Hull

The last part of the excavation was the removal of the hull. To accomplish this, archaeologists fabricated special tools, such as modified bottle jacks and nylon wedges, to gently pry timbers apart for removal. Even a large crane on the cofferdam wall was used at times to help separate larger timbers. The ship's remaining hull—about one third of the original—was dismantled plank-by-plank. All of the wood was soaked in water and special care was taken to protect it from drying out. All of the dismantled timbers were transported to the Conservation Research Laboratory at Texas A&M University's Riverside Campus in College Station, Texas.

Views of the hull, 1997
Courtesy Texas Historical Commission.

Artifact Conservation

Almost all of the artifacts from *La Belle* required conservation to preserve them. Wooden objects in particular can look quite sturdy when excavated but in reality can be very fragile. Much of the natural cellulose and lignin of the ship's wood had degraded and the void left had filled with seawater over time, which then became the primary agent for maintaining the artifact's shape. If the wood were to dry out, the cell walls would collapse and the artifact could shrink or warp. In some cases, further disintegration would take place and the original object would be completely unrecognizable.

Other materials require different conservation treatments. Ferrous materials (those containing iron) often are badly corroded—sometimes leaving little or none of the original metal. Electrolytic reduction can be used with metal that has not corroded too badly. The process involves placing the artifact into an alkaline electrolyte bath to convert some corroded products back to a metallic state. The result stabilizes the artifact from further degradation.

Conserving *La Belle*'s timbers, 1999
One of the jobs of the conservator is to prevent further damage to water-logged wood. The traditional method to preserve such objects is polyethylene glycol (PEG), a water-soluble synthetic wax. Wooden artifacts are immersed in this liquid until the PEG permeates the object and replaces the water. The PEG then forms the structure to maintain the original shape and look of the artifact. Another treatment for *La Belle*'s wood involves the use of silicone oil. The artifact is immersed in the oil and a crosslinker is added to tightly bond the oil with the object. The result is a very realistic-looking artifact that is less waxy than objects preserved with PEG. *Courtesy Texas Historical Commission.*

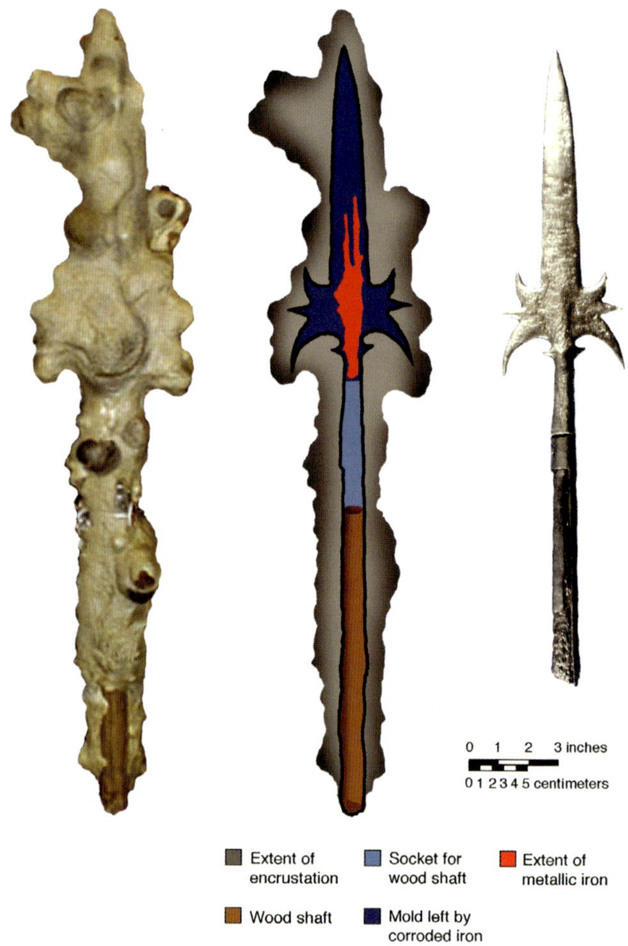

Illustration of artifact casting
Sometimes during immersion in seawater, a concretion will develop around an iron artifact before it corrodes away completely. The concretion forms because of an interaction between the corroding metal and the surrounding saltwater that causes the sediment in the seawater to be deposited around the artifact. This can create a near-perfect mold of the original object. Conservators can then open the concretion, clean out the interior mold, and pour epoxy into the void to make a cast of the original artifact. Many artifacts have been "recovered" in this way by the expert conservators at Texas A&M University's Conservation Research Laboratory. *Courtesy Texas Historical Commission.*

Conservation of the Hull

The single most important artifact from *La Belle* is the remains of the hull, and this has been the most complex object to preserve.

Polyethylene glycol (PEG) method, 2003
The initial plan was to use PEG to preserve the hull's wood timbers. A large concrete vat measuring 60 feet long, 20 feet wide, and 12 feet deep was built for this purpose. Later a top was constructed over the vat. The hull was reassembled and submerged into the vat of PEG. The plan was to start with a low molecular weight PEG and later change to a higher molecular weight PEG. The lower weight chemical is less viscous and readily permeates the wood to strengthen the cellular structure. The hull was immersed into this liquid and left to start preservation. As the time was nearing for the change to the higher molecular weight that would fill in additional areas to provide more strength, oil prices were spiking. As PEG is a hydrocarbon-based product, the cost of additional new PEG began to soar. *Courtesy Texas Historical Commission.*

Vacuum freeze-drying method, 2011

The amount of PEG needed to complete the preservation of the hull and its rising costs challenged conservators to find an alternative method, one that proved groundbreaking. Freeze-drying *La Belle* was suggested by Peter Fix, the chief conservator for the hull (shown left with freeze-dryer), and his colleagues. Freeze-drying as a means to preserve waterlogged artifacts has been in use since the early 1970s, but never on an artifact as large or complex as the hull of *La Belle*.

It was decided that after soaking in PEG for a shorter time, the ship would be disassembled. The timbers would then be individually placed into a freeze-dryer and the remaining water would be sublimated under a vacuum. During sublimation, water evaporates from a solid to a gas without going through the liquid stage. This process has several benefits. First, sublimation would prevent the differential drying of the timbers, which could cause shrinkage and warpage. Second, the final product would have a less waxy appearance than the pure PEG approach, and the wood would look more like the original hull timbers. And finally it would take three years less time to complete *La Belle*'s conservation. *Courtesy Conservation Research Laboratory, Texas A&M University, College Station.*

Essay Endnotes

European Competition for the New World

1. Alexander IV's donation and the Treaty of Tordesillas are placed in a North American context in David J. Weber, *The Spanish Frontier in North America* (New Haven: Yale University Press, 1992), 19–25.
2. A useful summary of the development of Spain's American empire and the competition it aroused among European rivals can be found in chapters 2 and 3 of Alan Taylor, *American Colonies* (New York: Viking, 2001), and early French failures in Canada are summarized on p. 92. An interesting exploration of the differences in European attitudes toward claiming sovereignty over New World territory is found in Patricia Seed, "Taking Possession and Reading Texts: Establishing the Authority of Overseas Empires," *The William and Mary Quarterly* 3rd ser., 49, no. 2 (April 1992): 183–209.
3. Spain's early problems with its European rivals are the subject of Kenneth R. Andrews, *Trade, Plunder, and Settlement: Maritime Enterprise and the Genesis of the British Empires, 1480–1630* (Cambridge: Cambridge University Press, 1984).
4. On New Netherlands and New Sweden, see Taylor, *American Colonies*, 251–57. A very readable summary of the European challenges to Spanish hegemony in the Caribbean in the course of the seventeenth century is found in part 2 of Jan Rogozinski, *A Brief History of the Caribbean: From the Arawak and Carib to the Present* (rev. ed., New York: Plume, 2000).
5. A very helpful and readable study focusing on the French-Spanish rivalry in Europe is J. H. Elliott, *Richelieu and Olivares* (Cambridge: Cambridge University Press, 1984). The development of French Canada is the subject of chapter 5 of Taylor, *American Colonies*.
6. The Spanish response to the La Salle episode and continued French challenges in North America from a Texas perspective can be found in Donald E. Chipman and Harriett Denise Joseph, *Spanish Texas, 1519–1821* (rev. ed., Austin: University of Texas Press, 2010), 99–112.

La Salle's 1684 Expedition

1. Information on La Salle's 1684 expedition to Texas is based primarily on Henri Joutel's journal account of the voyage found in Henri Joutel, *The La Salle Expedition to Texas: The Journal of Henri Joutel, 1684–1687*, ed. William C. Foster, trans. Johanna S. Warren (Austin: University of Texas Press, 1998). Information about the interest rates paid by La Salle can be seen in the journal by expedition engineer Jean-Baptiste Minet, "Journal of Our Voyage to the Gulf of Mexico," in *La Salle, the Mississippi, and the Gulf: Three Primary Documents*, ed. Robert S. Weddle, trans. Ann Linda Bell and Robert S. Weddle (College Station: Texas A&M University Press, 1987), 123.
2. For a comprehensive history of Nueva Vizcaya and the rich silver mines in the province, see Oakah L. Jones Jr., *Nueva Vizcaya, Heartland of the Spanish Frontier* (Albuquerque: University of New Mexico Press, 1988). Concerning a planned invasion of Spanish silver mines, see Beaujeu, Taneguy Le Gallois, "M. Beaujeu à Cabaret de Villermont," in *Découvertes et Établissements des Français dans l'Ouest et dans le Sud de l'Amérique Septentrinonale (1614–1754), Mémoires et Documents Originaux: Deuxième Partie, Lettres de Cavalier de La Salle et Correspondance Relative à Ses Entreprises (1678–1685)*, ed. Pierre Margry (Paris: Imprimérie de D. Jouaust, 1877), 426–31. "Mr. Beaujeu to Cabaret de Villermont" in *French Discoveries and Settlements in the West and in the South of North America (1614-1754)*, Memoirs and Original Documents: Part II, Letters of Cavalier de La Salle and Correspondence Relative to His Enterprises (1678–1685), ed. Pierre Margry, (Paris: Printing House of D. Jouaust, 1877), 426-431.
3. For an English translation of the expedition accounts of both Abbé Jean Cavelier and the priest Anastase Douay, see *Journeys of René Robert Cavelier, Sieur de La Salle,* vol. 1, ed. Isaac J. Cox (New York: A. S. Barnes and Company, 1905), 222–67; 268–98.
4. Information on La Salle's 1682 expedition down the Mississippi River is based primarily on the diary account of Nicolas de La Salle, *The La Salle Expedition on the Mississippi River: A Lost Manuscript of Nicolas de La Salle, 1682*, ed. William C. Foster, Trans. Johanna S. Warren (Austin: Texas State Historical Association, 2003). For information on the Marquette-Jolliet expedition down the Mississippi River in 1673, see Joseph P. Donnelly, *Jacques Marquette, S.J., 1637–1675* (Chicago: Loyola University Press, 1968).
5. Henri Joutel, *The La Salle Expedition to Texas: The Jour-*

nal of Henri Joutel, 1684–1687, ed. William C. Foster, trans. Johanna S. Warren (Austin: University of Texas Press, 1998), 57.

6. For information on the life of Dionisio Thomas, see Robert S. Weddle, *Wilderness Manhunt, The Spanish Search for La Salle* (Austin: University of Texas Press, 1973), 27–28, 87–88.
7. For a comprehensive review of maps of the Gulf of Mexico, including the 1684 Franquelin map, see Jack Jackson, *Flags Along the Coast, Charting the Gulf of Mexico, 1519–1759: A Reappraisal* (Austin: The Book Club of Texas, 1995). Also, see Peter Wood, "La Salle: Discovery of a Lost Explorer," *The American Historical Review* 89 2 (April 1984): 294–323.
8. Henri Joutel, *The La Salle Expedition to Texas: The Journal of Henri Joutel, 1684–1687*, ed. William C. Foster, trans. Johanna S. Warren (Austin: University of Texas Press, 1998) 57.

Native Americans

1. Lawrence E. Aten, *Indians of the Upper Texas Coast* (New York: Academic Press, 1983); Robert A. Ricklis, *The Karankawa Indians of Texas: An Ecological Study of Cultural Tradition and Change* (Austin: University of Texas Press, 1996), 5–8, 96, 171–72; Henri Joutel, *The La Salle Expedition to Texas: The Journal of Henri Joutel, 1684–1687*, ed. William C. Foster, trans. Johanna S. Warren (Austin: University of Texas Press, 1998), 94, 97, 117, 120, 147–48.
2. The eleven communities making up the Hasinai Confederacy were the Nacao, Nacachau, Nacono, Nechaui, Hainai, Neche, Nadaco (or Anadarko), Nabedache, Nabiti (or Namidish, Nawidish), Nacogdoche, and Nasoni. The Kadohadacho Confederacy included two Kadohadacho communities, as well as those of the Nanatsoho, Nasoni, and the upper Natchitoches. Lower Natchitoches, Ouachita, Yatasi, and Doustioni bands seem to have coalesced into the Natchitoches confederacy after 1700. Timothy K. Perttula, "The Great Kingdom of the Tejas: The Life and Times of Caddo Peoples in Texas between ca. 1530–1859," *Bulletin of the Texas Archeological Society* 72 (2001): 75; Timothy K. Perttula, *The Caddo Nation: Archaeological and Ethnohistoric Perspectives* (Austin: University of Texas Press, 1992), 85, 217–220; George Sabo, "The Structure of Caddo Leadership in the Colonial Era," in *The Native History of the Caddo: Their Place in Southeastern Archeology and Ethnohistory*, eds. Timothy K. Perttula and James E. Bruseth, Studies in Archeology 30 (Austin: Texas Archeological Research Laboratory, University of Texas at Austin, 1998); Juliana Barr, "Geographies of Power: Mapping Indian Borders in the 'Borderlands' of the Early Southwest," *The William and Mary Quarterly* 68, 1 (January 2011): 5–46; Juan Bautista Chapa, *Texas and Northeastern Mexico, 1630–1690*, ed. William C. Foster, trans. Ned F. Brierley (Austin: University of Texas Press, 1997), 138; Herbert E. Bolton, "The Spanish Occupation of Texas, 1519–1690," *Southwestern Historical Quarterly* 16, no. 1 (July 1912): 1–26: page 16 for quote.
3. Bishop of Guadalajara, *Informe*, 1676 as cited in Herbert Bolton, "The Spanish Occupation of Texas, 1519–1690," *Southwestern Historical Quarterly* 16 (July 1912): 16; Anastase Douay, "Narrative of La Salle's Attempt to Ascend the Mississippi in 1687," in *The Journeys of René Robert Cavelier, Sieur de la Salle*, 2 vols., ed. Isaac Joslin Cox (New York: AMS Press, 1973), 232, 231.
4. Nancy Hickerson, *The Jumanos: Hunters and Traders of the South Plains* (Austin: University of Texas Press, 1994); J. Charles Kelley, "Juan Sabeata and Diffusion in Aboriginal Texas," *American Anthropologist* 57 (October 1995): 981–95; Cecelia Sheridan, "Social Control and Native Territoriality in Northeastern New Spain," in *Choice, Persuasion, and Coercion: Social Control on Spain's North American Frontiers*, eds. Jesús F. de la Teja and Ross Frank, trans. Ned F. Brierley (Albuquerque: University of New Mexico Press, 2005), 126; Maria F. Wade, *The Native Americans of the Texas Edwards Plateau, 1582–1799* (Austin: University of Texas Press, 2003), 56.
5. Hickerson, *The Jumanos*.
6. This quote, and subsequent quotes from Joutel, are taken from his published diary.

Life and Death at Matagorda Bay

1. Joutel's diary records that La Salle left the temporary camp with forty to fifty men and left Joutel in camp with one hundred to one hundred and twenty individuals. See Henri Joutel, *The La Salle Expedition to Texas: The Journal of Henri Joutel, 1684–1687*, ed. William C. Foster, trans. Johanna S. Warren (Austin: University of Texas Press, 1998), 98.
2. Joutel notes that shortly after making landfall, two men were killed by Indians, several had deserted, and several died each day of various illnesses. See Joutel, *The La Salle Expedition*, 94, 97–98.

The Colony Kit

1. Louis Dieudonné de Bourbon,"Mémoire de Ce Qui Aura Esté Accordé au Sieur de La Salle,"*Découvertes et Établissements des Français dans l'Ouest et dans le Sud*

de l'Amérique Septentrinonale (1614–1754), Mémoires et Documents Originaux: Deuxième Partie, Lettres de Cavalier de La Salle et Correspondance Relative à Ses Entreprises (1678–1685), ed. Pierre Margry (Paris: Imprimérie de D. Jouaust, 1877), 378–80. Louis Dieudonné de Bourbon, "Memoir of What Was To Be Granted to the Sieur de La Salle," in *French Discoveries and Settlements in the West and in the South of North America (1614-1754)*, Memoirs and Original Documents: Part II, Letters of Cavalier de La Salle and Correspondence Relative to His Enterprises (1678–1685), ed. Pierre Margry, (Paris: Printing House of D. Jouaust, 1877), 378–80.

2. Joutel's journal was published in France in 1713: Henri Joutel, *Journal Historique du Dernier Voyage que feu M. de la Sale fit dans le Golfe de Mexique, pour trouver l'embouchure, & le cours de la Rivière de Missicipi, nommée à present la Rivière de Saint Loüis, qui traverse la Louisane; Où l'onvoit l'Histoire tragique de sa mort, & plusiers choses curieuses du nouveau monde; Par Monsieur Joutel, l'un des Compagnons de ce Voyage, redigé & mis en ordre par Monsier de Mitchel* (Paris: Chez Esatienne Robinot, Libraire, Quay &Attenant la Porte des Grands Augustins, à l'Angle Garien, 1713). An English version appeared the following year: Henri Joutel, *A Journal of the Last Voyage Perform'd by Monfr. de la Sale, to the Gulph of Mexico, to find out the Mouth of the Missisippi River; Containing An Account of the Settlements he endeavour'd to make on the Coast of the aforesaid Bay, his unfortunate Death, and the Travels of his Companions for the Space of Eight Hundred Leagues across that Inland Country of America, now call'd Louisiana, (and given by the King of France to M. Crozat,) till they came to Canada* (London: Printed for A. Bell at the Cross-Keys and Bible in Cornhill, B. Lintott at the Cross Keys in Fleet Street, and J. Baker in Pater-Noster-Row, 1714).

3. For more information about La Salle's mental state as argued by historians, see Robert S. Weddle, "Tarnished Hero: A La Salle Overview,"*Southwestern Historical Quarterly* vol. 113, no. 2 (October 2009): 158–83.

Discovery, Excavation, and Preservation

1. Information for this essay found in James E. Bruseth and Toni S. Turner, *From A Watery Grave: The Discovery and Excavation of La Salle's Shipwreck*, La Belle (College Station: Texas A&M University Press, 2005). Information about *La Belle* as a sailing ship is from Jean Boudriot, *Cavelier de La Salle, L'Expédition de 1684*, La Belle (Rotherfield, England: Jean Boudriot Publications, 2000).

Illustration Credits

Page 10. *La Salle Petitions the King for Permission to Explore the Mississippi.* From "The Great La Salle" by Henry Loomis Nelson, published in *Harper's Monthly Magazine*, February 1905. Oil on canvas by Howard Pyle. *Courtesy Delaware Art Museum, Wilmington, USA / The Bridgeman Art Library.*

Page 16. *Vue du Port de La Rochelle, prise de la petite Rive* (*View of the Port of La Rochelle, taken from the small bank*). Oil on canvas by Claude Joseph Vernet, ca. 1762. © *Musée national de la Marine/A. Fux.*

Page 36. Modern illustration of Karankawa. Illustration by Charles Shaw. *Courtesy Texas Historical Commission.*

Page 48. Modern illustration of La Salle leaving Fort St. Louis. Illustration by Charles Shaw. *Courtesy Texas Historical Commission.*

Page 92. Excavating *La Belle*, ca. 1996. Photograph by Robert Clark. *Courtesy Robert Clark and Texas Historical Commission.*

Acknowledgments

Many individuals have helped in the preparation of this catalog. David Denney and Joan Marshall offered me the opportunity to compile the exhibit catalog and have been a constant source of encouragement. Toni Turner, my wife and co-author of one of the catalog essays, offered advice on all phases of the catalog development and edited the text multiple times. Kathryn Siefker edited numerous drafts and suggested many modifications that have made the catalog better. Additional editing was undertaken by Amy Borgens, David Denney, Brad Jones, Pat Mercado-Allinger, Corinne Pignon, Miranda Smith, and Hélène Tromparent de Seynes. Glenn Grieco helped immensely with understanding the rigging artifacts recovered from the ship. To all of these people, I offer my sincerest thanks.

The information about the artifacts has come from studies conducted by many researchers. Much of the information is reported in James E. Bruseth and Toni S. Turner, *From A Watery Grave: The Discovery and Excavation of La Salle's Shipwreck,* La Belle (College Station: Texas A&M University Press, 2005). Additional information is from *La Belle: The Archeology of a 17th Century Ship of New World Colonization*, edited by James E. Bruseth, Amy Borgens, Bradford Jones, and Eric Ray (anticipated publication date is 2016). To the research team, I give my utmost appreciation for a job well done!

James E. Bruseth
May 2014

About the Guest Authors

Dr. Juliana Barr Associate Professor at the University of Florida. Dr. Barr specializes in the history of early America, the Spanish Borderlands, American Indians, and women and gender. Her book, *Peace Came in the Form of a Woman: Indians and Spaniards in the Texas Borderlands*, was published by the University of North Carolina Press in 2007.

Dr. James E. Bruseth Former Director of the Archeology Division at the Texas Historical Commission, which sponsored the excavation of *La Belle*, and guest curator for the Bullock Museum's *La Belle* project. Dr. Bruseth served as the Project Director for the excavation and recovery of *La Belle* and also directed the excavation of La Salle's Texas colony, Fort St. Louis. He has published numerous articles and monographs on the archaeology of Texas and the Southeast. His award winning book *From A Watery Grave: The Discovery and Excavation of La Salle's Shipwreck, La Belle*, was published by Texas A&M University Press and is the authoritative reference on the shipwreck of *La Belle*.

Jeffrey Durst Former Field Director for the Fort St. Louis site excavation. Durst is an archeologist with the Texas Historical Commission's South Texas Region and has been actively employed in archaeology for the past two decades.

William C. Foster Editor of *The La Salle Expedition to Texas: The Journal of Henri Joutel, 1684-1687*. Foster, an award-winning historian and fellow of the Texas State Historical Association, is also the author of *Spanish Expeditions Into Texas, 1689-1768* and *Historic Native Peoples of Texas*.

Dr. Jesús F. de la Teja Professor and Director of the Center for the Study of the Southwest, Texas State University-San Marcos. In February 2007, Governor Rick Perry appointed him to serve the first-ever, two-year term as State Historian of Texas. Dr. de la Teja has served as President of the Texas State Historical Association, and has written a number of books and articles on the history of Texas, Mexico, and Latin America.

Toni S. Turner Co-author of *From a Watery Grave: The Discovery and Excavation of La Salle's Shipwreck, La Belle*. An award-winning author, Turner is a former Development Officer at the Texas Historical Commission. She has worked on the *Belle* project since 1996 and has spent countless hours educating the public on the ship's significance.

Index